COL
MOUN
GUID

T0267192

COLORADO'S BEST HIKES FOR FALL COLORS

MATT ENQUIST

The Colorado Mountain Club Press

Golden, Colorado

Colorado's Best Hikes for Fall Colors
© 2023 by Matt Enquist

Published by:
The Colorado Mountain Club Press
710 10th Street, Suite 20, Golden, CO 80401
cmcpress@cmc.org | cmc.org/books

Corrections: We greatly appreciate when readers alert us to errors or outdated information
by contacting us at cmcpress@cmc.org.

Matt Enquist: photographer, except where noted
Vicki Hopewell: design and composition

Front cover: A sea of aspens below Capitol Peak (Hike 26).
Back cover: Climbing the Raccoon Trail (Hike 10).

Distributed to the book trade by:
Mountaineers Books
1001 SW Klickitat Way, Suite 201, Seattle, WA 98134
800-553-4453 | mountaineersbooks.org

We gratefully acknowledge the financial support of the people of Colorado
through the Scientific and Cultural Facilities District of greater metropolitan
Denver for our publishing activities.

TOPOGRAPHIC MAPS were created with CalTopo.com software.

Printed in Korea

ISBN 978-1-937052-62-1

23 24 25 / 10 9 8 7 6 5 4 3 2 1

WARNING AND DISCLAIMER
Read, Enjoy, and Proceed at your own Risk

To my Ritos

CONTENTS

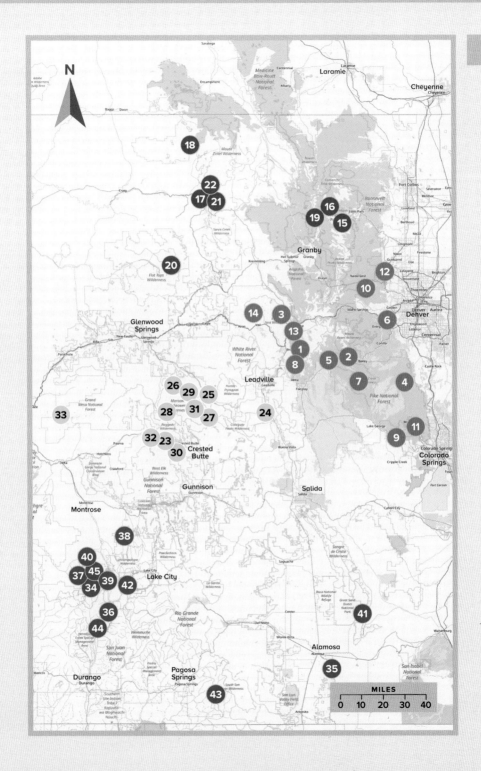

Raccoon Trail in Golden Gate
Canyon State Park (Hike 10).

INTRODUCTION

The fall has always been my favorite season. The cooler weather, the beauty of the changing leaves, the food, Oktoberfest brews . . . it all agrees with me. I look forward to September and October more than any other months.

Fall is a time for family, friends, and community—and I have always oriented my family, friends, and community around the outdoors. So, this book was a natural one for me to write. When fall rolls around, it's hard to keep me indoors. Hiking the trails during this best time of year is something truly special that I hope you too will enjoy.

Nature celebrates autumn with us. Animals are planning, preparing, traveling, and feasting just as we are. Plants are giving one last salute to the growth and change they worked hard on all summer. Hiking the trails in the fall feels like participating in a bigger picture. Enjoy it.

WHY DO LEAVES CHANGE?

Great question! As the temperatures cool in the fall, plants produce less and less chlorophyll. As the green-hued chlorophyll production slows, the other compounds present in the leaf year-round become more visible, each reflecting a different color of light back to our admiring eyes. Beta-carotene absorbs blue and green light, sending yellows and reds back to our eyes as orange leaves. Flavonols reflect the yellow fall color, while anthocyanin production increases in the fall, reflecting red to the hiker's eye.

WHAT IS THE BEST TIME TO SEE THE COLORS?

Each year brings a slightly different timeline for when the leaves will be at their peak color change. While that may be frustrating to the planner in you, finding out when and where to hike is easy enough with a little research in this guide and elsewhere. First, how do different factors play into the color change?

Generally, the northern parts of the state change color first, with the changing colors progressing southward. It may vary only by a few days but can make the difference between peak color and something less. Similarly, higher up on slopes tends to pop color before the bottoms of hills. The lower-elevation destinations may reach peak color later than the high peaks. Different slope faces and weather patterns also play a role year to year.

So, how do we plan around so many different variables? In the three years of writing this book, the last week of September and the first week of October have provided reliably beautiful tree color no matter where I went in the state.

I have noted any exceptions to that timeframe when writing individual chapters. There are also some external resources that will prove useful. Each year, meteorologists and members of the scientific forestry community chime in on that year's timeline on the news, be it on TV, online, or in the papers. Watch for reports on how that summer's precipitation and temperatures may affect the fall season you're looking to hike in.

Another great resource is smokymountains.com/fall-foliage-map/. This website is updated yearly with a sliding timeline animating a prediction of when leaves will be at their best across the entire nation, including Colorado! Inquiries to chambers of commerce, social media groups, and even webcams can also be great ways to scout the colors before grabbing this guide and heading to the hills.

THE SHOWSTOPPING PLANTS

Colorado in the fall is synonymous with the aspen tree. Colorado's ubiquitous *Populus tremuloides* (quaking aspen) is a beauty in all seasons, but it is the brilliant yellow (and less commonly) orange and red hues that make this the showstopper of Colorado fall. Aspen trees are clonal organisms, propagating through their roots to form genetically identical trees all as part of one living organism, connected underground.

Aspen groves can thus be seen as massive single organisms. In fact, the Kebler Pass aspen grove has laid claim to being the world's most massive organism. Aspen trees, the North American tree species with the widest natural distribution, live about one hundred years and reach 80 feet tall or more.

But the aspen tree is far from the only game in town when it comes to fall color. Colorado's multiple species of cottonwoods turn bright yellow, while urban hardwood trees resemble the spectacle put on farther east in the country. Ash trees and box elders add to the show, while various species of willow pop yellow colors along creek beds statewide. And don't forget about the grasses and forbs both above and below tree line. Almost all of them play a part in the fall color spectacle across the few months of fall.

I have tried to call out specific species visible on different hikes. However, I am no botanist. I would recommend hiking with a small field guide or pamphlet to get the most out of your plant identification experience, if that's part of what gets you on the trail.

NOTES ON HIKE SELECTIONS

Writing "the *best* forty-five hikes for fall colors" may be impossible. There are surely hundreds of hikes I've never even heard of that merit consideration. So, I sought to write up forty-five hikes that will appeal to a wide variety of hikers with one thing that unites them all: noteworthy beauty, specifically in the fall, as well as the opportunity for adventure. Also note that this guide is focused on day hikes, as opposed to backpacking loops, although where an easy loop for an overnight trip is available, I have noted it in the chapter text.

People hike for a lot of different reasons. Some climb the highest peaks and look to get the adrenaline coursing. Others look for animals, identify plants, or simply watch the sky. I sought to appeal to a wide audience.

Vibrant colors seen from the trailhead at Interlaken—Twin Lakes (Hike 24).

Also note that there is only one "14er" summit in this guide. This is not a commentary on 14er culture or any slight to those hikes. Instead, 14,000-foot peaks are often covered in snow during long parts of the fall. That being said, tundra grass hikes are well represented in this guide, and those looking to climb a 14er, with proper scouting of the weather and hiker fitness, should enjoy those high peaks and thin air with confidence (for example, check out the east slopes of Mount Elbert)!

I regret not being able to include hikes on the eastern plains. Pawnee Buttes to the north and the Comanche National Grassland (anyone want to witness a tarantula migration?!) to the south stick out in particular as fantastic options for fall hiking when the temperatures cool down and much of the high-country color has fallen off the trees.

ARBORGLYPHS

There are references to arborglyphs throughout this book, and I encourage you to read about them in the specific chapters. I find these historical carvings on trees fascinating. That being said, these are historical, culturally significant carvings. Don't carve trees! I've seen too many beautiful groves defaced with "John was here" or even political views. Don't do it.

HOW TO USE THIS GUIDE

Ratings

Trail difficulty ratings are based on a number of factors. I've attempted to create an apples-to-apples comparison across all hikes in this book. However, we all experience difficulty differently. Some people fly uphill while others struggle. Some dread the knee-pounding descents while others sprint downhill. So, I've attempted to describe my rationale for difficulty rankings in each hike write-up. These are among the factors determining hike difficulties:

Round-trip distance: Generally, longer hikes are rated as harder hikes.
Elevation gain: How high are you going to be climbing, and how fast do you have to do it? The steepness of the climb is often the most telling factor for me when ranking hikes.
Trail conditions: Do you have to hunt for the trail, or is it wide and clear to the naked eye? Am I about to send you scrambling over boulders, or is the trail ahead as smooth as a sidewalk?

Round-Trip Time

The time required to complete a hike will differ from person to person. I tend to be a fast hiker, but I did not record my hiking times for each chapter. When estimating the time required to do these hikes, I attempted to give a time that an average-speed hiker would take to finish the trek. Those who hike fast, out of habit or personal challenge, will naturally finish these routes quicker than those who want to listen to the leaves crunch a little more.

A hiker's physical fitness will obviously play a role in how quickly they finish a trail. And remember that you are only as fast as the slowest member of your group. Also take into account that hikes in this guide are all over the spectrum for elevation. Some people have a much harder time, physically, dealing with altitude than others. If you're coming from a lower elevation to hike, listen to your body, and take the time to get acclimated before endeavoring to push your limits on a trail.

Driving Directions

I wrote driving directions to trailheads based on the nearest town. However, consult your own navigation devices and research your route on the way to trailheads. Road names change, new routes are constructed, and other roads close. Do your due diligence before jumping in the car.

LEAVE NO TRACE

Tread lightly—leave the areas you visit better than you found them. The Leave No Trace ethic outlined below was developed to provide guidelines for using and enjoying the outdoors responsibly:

Camp on durable surfaces and never cut switchbacks. If you decide to go off trail, groups should spread out instead of walking single file to avoid trampling vegetation into new trails.

Respect wildlife. If an animal appears agitated by your presence, you're probably too close.

Dispose of waste in a responsible manner. Pack it in, pack it out.

Be careful with fires. Much of the state is a tinderbox. Please be careful with your campfires, research and obey burn warnings and prohibitions, and consider foregoing a fire altogether in the backcountry when camping. Drown your fires before leaving them.

Maintain the silence of the backcountry. Keep radios at home and keep conversation from disturbing animals or other visitors.

The upper reaches of the Opal Lake hike are colorful and mostly flat (Hike 43).

HIKING PRECAUTIONS

Fall is hunting season. Wear bright clothing. Tie a blaze-orange bandana around your pack or wear some hunting-orange clothing. Hikers share the land with many other users in fall, and the safe and responsible way to use the land is to be visible.

Always leave your expected itinerary with a friend or family member who is not on the trail with you. Let them know when you expect to return. Consider investing in a satellite communicator of some sort if you are a frequent backcountry user. Be conservative in your decision-making and always be honest about your limitations.

All backcountry water should be treated using a purifier or filter to avoid illness. Never drink untreated water, no matter how clean and pure it may appear.

WEATHER

While the fall season in Colorado tends to have more stable weather than the summer (when hikers need to constantly be vigilant for afternoon storms rolling in), the same rules still apply for hikers watching the weather. Keep an eye out for thunderstorms, particularly when you find yourself at higher altitudes or in exposed areas. Snow is possible at any time and is quite common in the fall-leaf season. Dress for all possible weather! Alternatively, heat can be a concern. Drink plenty of water and wear sun protection.

THE TEN ESSENTIALS

The Ten Essentials "systems" can be credited to *Mountaineering: The Freedom of the Hills*, a must-own book for anyone who loves traveling in the mountains and wants to do it safely.

1. **Navigation (map and compass).** Carry an up-to-date map and an accurate compass, and know how to use them. I hike with a GPS as well as a map and compass.
2. **Sun protection (sunglasses and sunscreen).** The sun can sap your energy and motivation surprisingly quickly. Lather up and protect yourself every day.
3. **Insulation (extra clothing).** Carry enough insulation to keep you warm in any condition you might reasonably experience, no matter how close to the car you plan on being. Carry reliable rain gear and protect your supplies from water. Avoid cotton clothing, which absorbs water and resists drying.
4. **Illumination (headlamp/flashlight).** A quality headlamp (with extra batteries) should have a place in every daypack or overnight kit. Don't get caught in an emergency situation made worse by a lack of visibility.
5. **First aid supplies.** Carry and stock a first aid kit suitable for your size group. Know how and when to use the supplies and how to make informed decisions about medical situations in the backcountry. A Wilderness First Aid (WFA) course is a highly recommended first-step investment in yourself.
6. **Fire (waterproof matches/lighter/candles).** If you need a fire to stay warm, know how to start and maintain one.
7. **Repair kit and tools.** Carrying gear patches, extra buckles, and cord is always a wise choice.
8. **Nutrition (extra food).** Prepare for the worst-case scenario.
9. **Hydration (extra water).** Consume plenty of water and consider bringing a water filter or purifying tablets on longer hikes.
10. **Emergency shelter.** For the day hiker, a bivy sack or other emergency shelter is a wise choice. They're light and packable and may very well make the difference for you if you end up stranded overnight.

Knowledge. Perhaps most essential of all, in addition to that listed above, is an up-to-date knowledge of your upcoming trip. Do your homework, be conservative, and have fun.

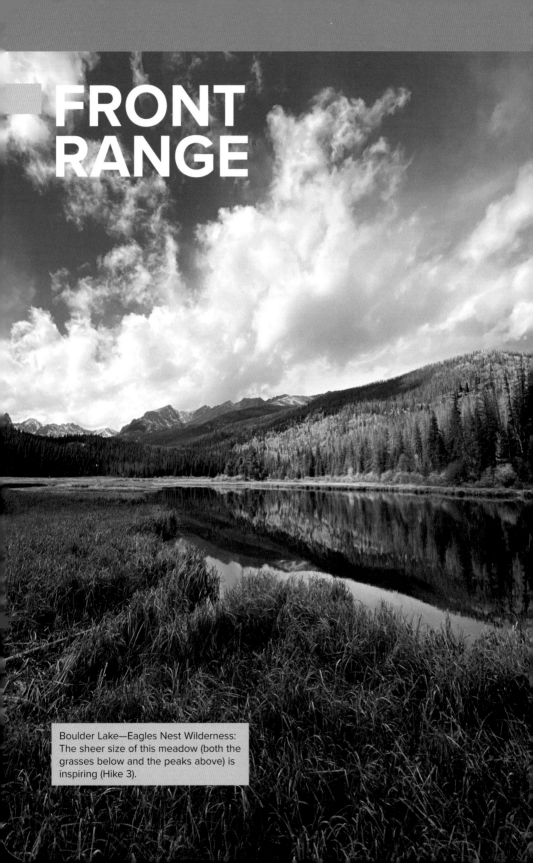

FRONT RANGE

Boulder Lake—Eagles Nest Wilderness: The sheer size of this meadow (both the grasses below and the peaks above) is inspiring (Hike 3).

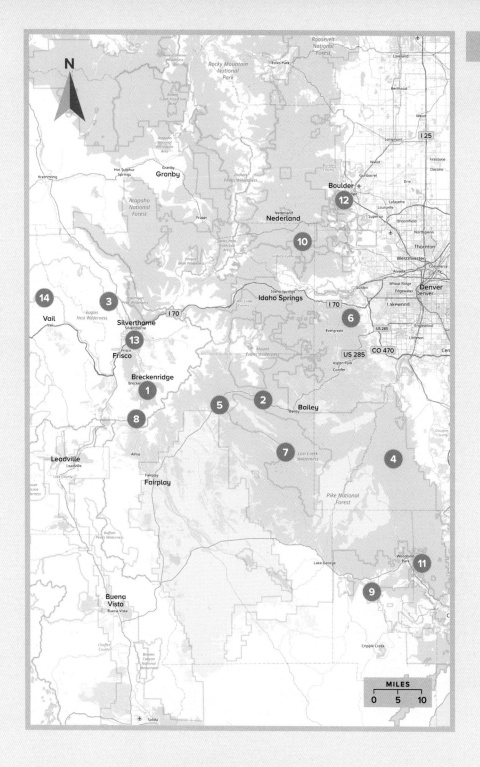

ASPEN ALLEY

1

Rating	Moderate
Round-Trip Distance	3 miles
Elevation Gain	515 feet
Round-Trip Time	2 hours
Maps	Trails Illustrated 109: Breckenridge, Tennessee Pass
Main Attraction	A tunnel of aspen trees, some history, and the opportunity to make this a point-to-point trail or a round-trip

COMMENT: Any trail called Aspen Alley promises to bring plenty of fall color, and the lower reaches of this trail do not disappoint.

GETTING THERE: From Breckenridge, drive south on South Main Street and turn left onto Boreas Pass Road. Continue for 1.1 miles and turn right onto Illinois Gulch Road. Climb Illinois Gulch Road for 0.7 mile, then turn left on Bunker Hill Road. Turn right back onto Boreas Pass Road and continue 0.5 mile to the trailhead.

As expected, dense stands of aspen grace Aspen Alley.

COLORADO'S BEST HIKES FOR FALL COLORS

Left: Local ski resorts are lucky to be surrounded by so much fall beauty. **Right:** The bottom portions of the hike provide long views and plenty of color.

TRAILHEAD: The Boreas Pass Trailhead is a small, muddy collection of parking spots that serves as a launching-off point for a number of local-favorite trails.

THE ROUTE: From the Boreas Pass Trailhead, hike to the west end of the parking lot and climb briefly up the road past a metal gate. On your right (north), there is a small post sign for the Aspen Alley Trail. It can be a bit easy to miss, so keep a sharp eye out for the small trail diving off the right side of the road.

A third of a mile after leaving the car, the trail enters the first batch of aspen color and continues gently downward. The trail begins to show signs of mining and sawmill uses from enterprises long past. At 1 mile, there is an abandoned mine cart on tracks coming out of a culvert.

The trail descends through a tranquil pine forest on a solid packed dirt (or mud, depending on recent rain or snowfall) surface. The descent through pines undulates back and forth and occasionally brings you into contact with some private property. Make sure you're staying on the public lands and respecting the property lines.

Continue descending through aspens so dense that the views off the hillside are sometimes fully obstructed by aspen trunks. When the view does open up, the trail affords views of Breckenridge Ski Resort and the majestic Tenmile Range. The

The top portions of the trail in particular provide panoramic views.

domed peak on the left is Mount Helen, while the peak towering above the ski runs on the right is Peak 10.

At 1.2 miles, more evidence of industrial use is visible with the presence of a large boiler, long since abandoned to the elements. Enjoy even better views of the Tenmile Range with aspens lighting up the lower reaches and snow dusting the pinnacles.

At 1.5 miles, the hike bottoms out at the Breckenridge Sawmill Museum, home to the sawyers' cabins, the original sawmill, and some informational pamphlets. The early history of Breckenridge was driven by sawmills such as this, which allowed the economy and town to grow large enough to house miners and a booming population. Along with that came schools, stores, churches, and the like. The museum allows for a self-guided tour via QR code on a smartphone.

From here, you can hike back up the trail you just descended (the basis for the 3-mile round-trip figure quoted in this guide), or you can take the road to the northeast, out of the Sawmill, and climb the Illinois Gulch Road that you drove in on to get back to your car.

Alternately, if there are multiple cars in your group, you can station one car at the top and one at the Sawmill Museum and do this as a shuttle hike. Whether you prefer to descend or ascend in that situation is up to you. If you do decide to leave a car at the Sawmill Museum, make sure to follow all parking regulations and do not block the private driveways and access road that leaves the lot.

ASPEN ALLEY

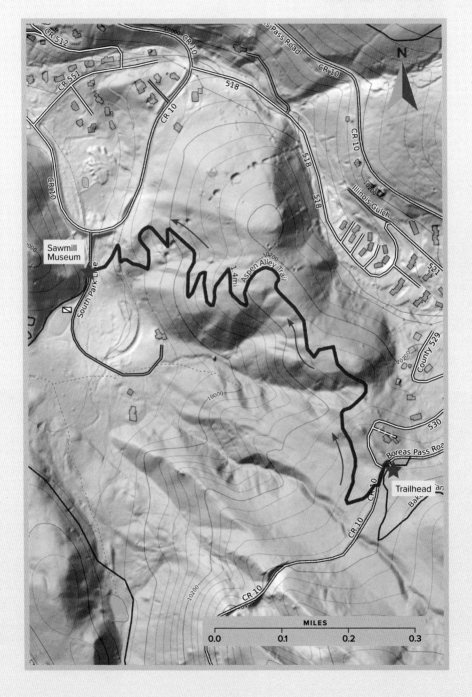

BEN TYLER TRAIL

2

Rating	Difficult
Round-Trip Distance	12.5 miles
Elevation Gain	3,700 feet
Round-Trip Time	8 hours
Maps	Trails Illustrated 105: Tarryall Mountains, Kenosha Pass
Main Attraction	A difficult hike close to the Front Range with views of a huge aspen grove

COMMENT: One of the Front Range's best hikes for fall color, the Ben Tyler Trail ascends steeply into a massive aspen grove before topping out at a high saddle with sweeping vistas.

GETTING THERE: The Ben Tyler Trail is located 6.8 miles west of Bailey on the south side of US Highway 285. The trailhead is marked by a small brown sign on the south side of the road and is often quite busy.

Left: The trail passes through deep ruts in an old aspen grove. **Right:** Dense aspen trees can make the trail dark at times.

The upper reaches of the trail afford views of the yellow aspen grove as a whole.

TRAILHEAD: The Ben Tyler Trailhead has parking for around fifteen vehicles and is very close to the highway. Use caution when leaving the trailhead as traffic on US 285 is moving fast! The trail starts at the east end of the parking shoulder.

THE ROUTE: The trail begins on the edge of the highway and immediately gains 300 feet over the course of twelve switchbacks and 0.4 mile. Above the switchbacks, leave the sounds of the road behind and continue to climb through ponderosa pines before leveling off and traversing more open terrain along a trail flanked by mountain mahogany bushes (look for their incredible curly seed tails in the fall and winter) and offering views of Ben Tyler Gulch above. At 1.3 miles, sign in to the wilderness area at the register box and enter a forested section of trail soon thereafter. At 1.6 miles, the trail nearly touches the creek and offers a junction to some camping options. Do not cross the creek and instead continue uphill.

Lost in a yellow canopy.

From here, the trail steepens on often-rocky trails before finally crossing the creek at 2 miles. The trail begins to ascend even more rapidly here but soon puts you in a massive aspen grove that can feel like a hallway of yellow leaves from mid-September onward. As the trees periodically open up, you'll catch glimpses of the other side of the hill covered in aspens.

At 10,580 feet and 4 miles from the trailhead, the first set of switchbacks begins. For the next half mile, you will be rewarded with sweeping views back down the gulch, filled with aspens. After this, the trail goes from a "moderate" endeavor to a "difficult" one, and the aspen show fades into the background in favor of an approach to the tundra. Turn back if you were only in it for the fall colors or continue if you want the alpine views.

The second of three sets of switchbacks begins at 4.8 miles, and the trail meets up with the Craig Park Trail at 5 miles. Stay to the right to continue climbing the Ben Tyler Trail. Traverse the final set of switchbacks at 5.5 miles, winding through bristlecone pines before emerging onto the alpine tundra at the 6-mile mark. The rolling saddle offers views of South Park and the Collegiate Peaks to the southwest and Mounts Evans and Bierstadt to the north. Return the way you came.

I rated this trail "difficult" because of the steep climbs in the middle of the hike. The terrain is often rocky and loose. Routefinding above tree line can get slightly complicated as multiple social trails crisscross the landscape and official trails branch off to other parts of the wilderness area. The round-trip hike is lengthy and requires you to assess the fitness and stamina of the group.

If you are looking to make a fantastic day hike into a backpacking trip, this is an ideal option that can combine multiple colorful hikes into a single adventure. Combine the Ben Tyler Trail up over the Kenosha Mountains. From the top of this hike, it is possible to descend Ben Tyler Gulch on the south side of the mountains until it meets the Colorado Trail. Continue west to the Kenosha Pass hike listed in Hike 5. Stationing one car at Kenosha Pass and another at the Ben Tyler Trailhead would make an easy point-to-point 17.8-mile hike that combines two fantastically colorful hikes close to the Front Range.

BEN TYLER TRAIL

BOULDER LAKE— EAGLES NEST WILDERNESS

3

Rating	Moderate to difficult
Round-Trip Distance	5.6 miles
Elevation Gain	1,527 feet
Round-Trip Time	4 hours
Maps	Trails Illustrated 108: Vail, Frisco, Dillon
Main Attraction	A relatively easily accessible alpine lake, ringed with peaks and aspens

COMMENT: You should have to work harder to get to an alpine lake of this caliber. Rarely can hikers get to such a majestic lake with such little effort.

GETTING THERE: From Silverthorne, drive north on Colorado Highway 9 for roughly 7.5 miles. Turn left (west) onto County Road 1350 and climb the solid dirt road. Climb for 1.3 miles, then turn left to continue toward the Rock Creek Trail-

Boulder Lake on a placid day.

The peaks of Eagles Nest Wilderness loom large over Boulder Lake.

head. The road gets more rugged and rocky from here, but most passenger cars should be able to make it to the trailhead at 1.6 miles.

TRAILHEAD: The Rock Creek Trailhead is a loop with plenty of parking. Arrive early, however, as this is a very popular hike, for good reason. There are no restrooms.

THE ROUTE: From the Rock Creek Trailhead, climb the rocky trail to the Eagles Nest Wilderness boundary. Register at the free entry station if you are staying overnight. Climb the wide gravel trail as it ascends casually for 0.3 mile to the turnoff for Boulder Lake. Turn right at the sign to ascend the mountainside toward the lake.

From here, the trail gets narrower and rockier, climbing gently at first. Undulate through the ups and downs of a marshy area and watch for wildlife in the meadows below. Across the valley is the Ptarmigan Peak Wilderness, with aspens lighting up the hillside below.

The trail proceeds through a brief flat section before climbing through a beetle-kill forest. The climb up here is moderate in slope but unrelenting in its persistence, climbing nearly 500 vertical feet from the turnoff with the parking-lot trail.

There is plenty of fun here for hikers who love a dense aspen forest.

The high-point elevation comes on a narrow ridge at 1.75 miles. Enjoy big views into the Eagles Nest Wilderness to the south and west of the Ptarmigan Peaks (over the Eisenhower Tunnel) to the east.

From this high point, descend steeply in a pine forest that is less affected by beetle kill. The trail descends through switchbacks and fewer aspen views and becomes rocky until it bottoms out at 2.4 miles and a wooden bridge over the creek emanating from the Boulder Lake saddle above.

Turn left after the log bridge to climb toward Boulder Lake. The brief climb to the lake has a number of social trails leading to campsites above and views of the small waterfalls below. I stayed as close to the creek as possible without taking a dead-end social trail to a view of the creek.

Continue toward the lake amid yellow undergrowth, until emerging on the majestic Boulder Lake at 2.8 miles. I have undertaken few hikes in this state that required less effort than this one to reach such a majestic alpine lake as this one.

The lake itself is shallow, though full of decent sized fish, with a marshy border surrounding it. The north side of the lake is ringed with aspens. Of the peaks towering above the lake, only the far-left mountain is named: Keller Mountain. The Eagles Nest Wilderness is a rugged place, full of beautiful peaks with only elevation numbers for their names.

Take your time marveling at the peaks, the water, and the color. Return the way you came.

I rated this hike "moderate to difficult" because I believe it falls between the moderate and difficult designations listed in this guide. It is a slightly longer round trip than some of the moderate hikes here, but the elevation gain and distance do not quite make it overly difficult. Start early, take it slow, and gauge your stamina if you are pushing the limits of your group. But this is truly one of the more beautiful alpine destinations in this humble guide.

BOULDER LAKE—
EAGLES NEST WILDERNESS

DEVIL'S HEAD LOOKOUT

4

Rating	Moderate
Round-Trip Distance	2.75 miles
Elevation Gain	950 feet
Round-Trip Time	2.5 hours
Maps	Trails Illustrated 135: Deckers, Rampart Range
Main Attraction	An iconic Front Range hike to a historic fire lookout

COMMENT: The ever-popular Devil's Head Lookout hike is close to Denver and Colorado Springs and offers panoramic views of the foothills alight with aspen color.

GETTING THERE: From Castle Rock (a launching-off point for Denver and Colorado Springs residents, but consult a GPS of your choice for your own directions),

There are 143 stairs up to the panoramic lookout.

Left: The Devil's Head Lookout is the oldest functioning fire lookout in Colorado. **Right:** The fire lookout provides long views in all directions.

drive west on Wolfensberger Road for 8.5 miles to Colorado Highway 105 south (Perry Park Road). Turn right onto Rampart Range Road. Follow the winding dirt Rampart Range Road for 12 miles to the Devil's Head Lookout Trailhead.

TRAILHEAD: The Devil's Head Lookout Trailhead is a large but crowded parking area with restrooms. Due to the popularity of this hike, the bathrooms and other facilities in this area can get trashed. Please take care of this area! Pick up after yourself.

THE ROUTE: Start at the stone stairs at the south end of the parking area, where you'll begin your steady climb to the panoramic views ahead. The first section of the hike takes you through a patch of raspberry plants (some may still be hanging on to a late-season berry or two) and the damage from a rare tornado that hit this area in 2015.

Keep climbing into the area's characteristic granite boulders and formations. The granite here is pink to red. The color comes from the high feldspar and iron contents of the rocks. The rock is crumbly and full of large-grained crystals. The rock here is a subset to Pikes Peak granite, the type of stone that makes up the iconic 14,155-foot peak 30 miles to the south.

Devil's Head Lookout

Patches of fall color are sprinkled throughout the foreground and background views.

At 0.75 mile, the trail climbs on a section of metal laid into concrete to increase traction and help with trail erosion. Continue to climb through switchbacks. The trail here is mostly through a pine forest with occasional views to the west. There are a few picnic tables and scenic spots for a break.

At 1.25 miles, the trail passes through a cut in the rocks as it nears the top of the trail. The top of the hike is at 1.35 miles, where the trail empties you into a small flat area with seasonal restrooms, a closed Forest Service cabin, and the staircase up to the main event: the historic fire lookout. Climb the 143 steep stairsteps up to the lookout.

The top of the stairs features a boardwalk surrounding the working part of the lookout. The panoramic views are breathtaking, with fall colors dotting the hillsides in every direction. The colors are beautiful from the top, but part of the appeal of hiking this trail in the fall is to avoid some of the summer crowds and higher temperatures on this justifiably popular hike.

The fire lookout has been an actively staffed Forest Service lookout for over a hundred years. Fire lookouts were once more common and played a part in spotting forest fires and dispatching wildland fire crews. The Devil's Head Lookout still plays an important role in protecting the Front Range from wildfire.

The Devil's Head Lookout was also the first station in Colorado to have a female fire lookout, Helen Dowe, in 1919. Today, dedicated employees still work here. Visitors are welcome to walk around the deck on the lookout, but be respectful of Forest Service employees on the job.

The trail was built in 1933 by the Civilian Conservation Corps as part of Franklin Delano Roosevelt's New Deal. The trail was partially rebuilt and the modern staircase still in place today was installed in 1951.

I rated this hike "moderate" because of its steep climb but short mileage. The trail is well maintained and has good footing with plenty of stops to take a break. Enjoy the top and return the way you came to the trailhead.

DEVIL'S HEAD LOOKOUT

COLORADO TRAIL— KENOSHA PASS

5

Rating	Easy
Round-Trip Distance	4 miles
Elevation Gain	500 feet
Round-Trip Time	3 hours
Maps	Trails Illustrated 105: Tarryall Mountains, Kenosha Pass
Main Attraction	Easily accessible, very dense aspen forests

COMMENT: One of the premiere fall hikes for Denver and Colorado Springs residents, this hike is an easily accessible, casual hike through a low-alpine aspen grove.

GETTING THERE: From Denver, drive west on US 285. Pass through the towns of Bailey and Grant, and begin to climb Kenosha Pass. At the pass, there are parking areas on the east and west sides of the road with signage for the pass and the Colorado Trail.

Left: Kenosha Pass is a favorite fall hike of so many in the Front Range. **Right:** Kenosha Pass has one of the densest aspen groves nearest to Denver.

The hillsides above Kenosha Pass.

TRAILHEAD: The Kenosha Pass Colorado Trail parking area spans both sides of the road with parking spots along the road. In the busy fall season, even all of these spots can be filled. Arrive early to beat the crowds. It may be possible to park in the Kenosha Pass Campground east of the road, but this hike is written as if the gate were closed, and the trail starts at the pass.

THE ROUTE: From the east side of the pass, hike a third of a mile down the road toward the old railroad tracks. The Colorado Trail starts opposite the informational signs. The trail climbs through a very dense aspen grove parallel to the highway but with enough distance to make this a tranquil, quiet hike.

The dirt trail alternates between double- and single-track dirt trails. Battle the crowds but don't forget to savor the views through the aspens of the dense forest on the other side of Kenosha Pass and over the majestic South Park.

At 1 mile, enter an older aspen grove. The bigger trees tower above the well-trodden trail before entering a burn scar with young trees at 1.4 miles. Again enjoy majestic views over South Park and the rest of the Kenosha Pass aspen grove.

From here, the trail climbs steeper to a panoramic open spot at 2 miles. This is an ideal spot to enjoy lunch or simply a moment to admire the big views over South Park.

Enjoy the view and turn back the way you came. Or continue onward into the Lost Creek Wilderness. The possibilities are endless in this part of the state. It is possible to connect to the Ben Tyler Trail (Hike 2) or the Wigwam Trail (Hike 7), both described in this guidebook.

I rated this hike "easy" because of its short distance and mild elevation gains. Also, even if you turn around early, this hike is still a winner. The appeal of this hike is the ability to walk in such a dense grove of mature aspen trees so close to such major metropolitan areas.

There are excellent dispersed camping sites off Lost Park Road, just south of Kenosha Pass, if you choose to make this an overnight trip from the nearby major cities. Traffic can be an issue heading home from either side of the pass if you visit on a weekend.

Kenosha Pass is the gateway to the west side of the majestic Lost Creek Wilderness. Make the stop at Kenosha Pass just the beginning of a station-to-station trip enjoying the best fall color close to both Colorado Springs and Denver.

This is also a popular waypoint on the Colorado Trail. The Colorado Trail takes hikers from Waterton Canyon, outside of Denver, to Durango. The trail travels 486 miles, passing through some of the most majestic parts of the state. Take a moment to enjoy this small but gorgeous segment of the trail.

The classic fencing alongside the hike starting from US 285.

COLORADO TRAIL—KENOSHA PASS

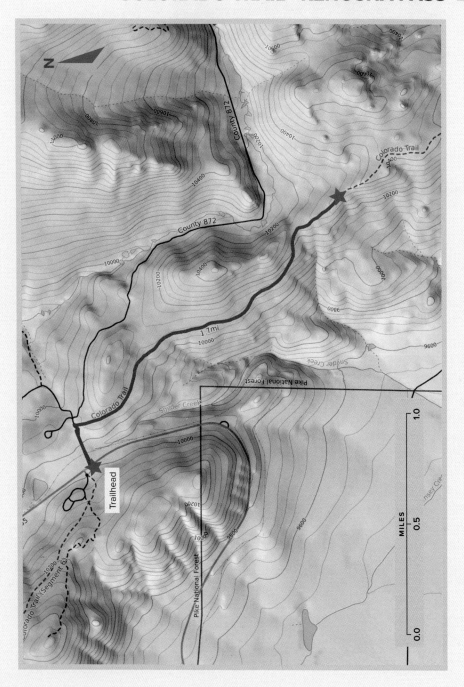

LAIR O' THE BEAR PARK   6

Rating	Easy
Round-Trip Distance	1.6 miles
Elevation Gain	340 feet
Round-Trip Time	1 hour
Maps	Trails Illustrated 100: Boulder, Golden; trail maps also available at the trailhead
Main Attraction	A Front Range paradise of cottonwoods, fruit trees, and post-hike breweries

COMMENT: Close to Denver, the Lair o' the Bear is a fun late-season hike that's flat, beautiful, and adventurous all at the same time.

GETTING THERE: From Denver, depending on where you're coming from, head west on Interstate 70 to Colorado Highway 470 south. Take the exit for the town of

Riverside cottonwoods begging to be climbed.

Left: The Lair o' the Bear Trail circles around the creek. **Right:** Mountain mahogany seeds.

Morrison and continue on the road through town for 5 miles up into the canyon above Morrison. Be cautious driving through Morrison as this is a bustling tourist town full of pedestrians. Turn left into the Lair o' the Bear Park parking area south of the road.

TRAILHEAD: Lair o' the Bear Open Space Park has one parking area just off the highway. Despite a plethora of parking spaces, get there early to get a space on weekends and holidays!

THE ROUTE: From the spacious but bustling parking area, walk south under the canopy of narrowleaf cottonwoods toward Bear Creek. As the trail gets close to the creek, turn left (east) to continue on the creekside trail. There are a number of social trails in this area, as this is a very popular urban trail, but continue hiking east along the creek. The trail meanders along the creek and dense riparian creekside vegetation before drifting away from the creek then turning south to meet the creek again.

Where the trail is about to cross the creek, there is one of the most impressive cottonwood trees in the Front Range. Marvel at the expansive branches of this creekside specimen and enjoy one of the many picnic spots by the creek bridge.

After 0.25 mile, the trail moves on from the landmark cottonwood tree and crosses the creek on a wide, sturdy bridge. A third of a mile from the trailhead, turn

Creekside color.

right (west) at the sign and begin to climb below a small cliff. The trail climbs gently into a stand of aspens. At 0.5 mile, stay left to climb higher on the Bruin Bluff Trail.

From here, the trail switchbacks casually on the hillside before revealing expansive views of the creek below, flush with fall colors. The trail soon approaches a high point with shallow-angle cliffs and a diversity of plant life typical of the Rocky Mountain foothills.

From here, descend in a shady pine forest. Continue on to the bridge at 1.4 miles and turn right (east) to return to the parking area after 1.5 miles.

The main reason I love this trail, other than the convenience to the big city, is the diversity of plant life. The predominant tall trees are narrowleaf cottonwoods. Narrowleaf cottonwood is a species of cottonwood distinct from the broad-leafed plains cottonwood and grows more in the foothills and foothills canyons than in the sweltering lower-elevation plains. Along the creek side, stands of chokecherry trees grow thick. Other noteworthy plant species are the thick shrubs with the incredible spiral-shaped seeds. Mountain mahogany seeds are a beautiful feathery spiral, plentiful and beautiful in the fall season. Serviceberries periodically steal the show with their bright-red leaves, and there are even a couple apple trees remaining on the property, perhaps leftover from some creekside homestead.

I rated this hike "easy" for its short distance, well-traveled and easy-to-navigate path, and docile elevation changes. The trail does get a bit rocky on the west side of the loop, but the inclines and declines are generally moderate and easy to navigate. This is a fantastic family hike for those with kids or guests from out of town. For someone who loves plants and appreciates the diversity of the fall landscape, this hike is a relaxing trip through a riparian foothill environment, close to the big city and a lot of great breweries nearby.

LAIR O' THE BEAR PARK

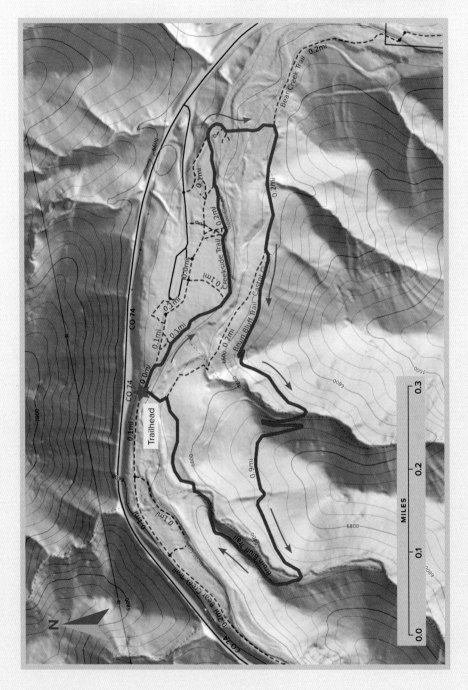

THE WIGWAM TRAIL— LOST PARK TRAILHEAD

7

Rating	Easy to moderate
Round-Trip Distance	10.5 miles
Elevation Gain	150 feet
Round-Trip Time	5 hours
Maps	Trails Illustrated 105: Tarryall Mountains, Kenosha Pass
Main Attraction	Golden willows and foraging moose

COMMENT: This scenic hike is remarkable for its consistently flat trail that weaves back and forth between shady forests and open meadows with enticing rock faces watching over moose browsing below.

GETTING THERE: The Lost Park Trailhead is located at the end of the 19-mile Lost Park Road east of the town of Jefferson. From Denver, take US 285 west for

Hiking the high meadow full of willow and understory color.

Left: The upper reaches of the valley. **Right:** There are plenty of picnic rocks toward the upper ends of the valley.

68 miles, crossing over Kenosha Pass and heading toward the small town of Jefferson. Just before entering town, look for the brown Forest Service sign pointing you down Lost Park Road. Continue straight on the well-graded dirt road (not maintained in winter), ignoring the numerous offshoots to dispersed camping spots and gated detours. Follow the signs for the Lost Park Campground and Trailhead. The trailhead is located on the east end of the lower campground loop and has a modest parking lot for hikers.

TRAILHEAD: The Lost Park Trailhead is just outside the paid campground. Snag a site and spend the night or park outside the gate and hike without having to pay.

THE ROUTE: The hike begins at the trailhead at the end of the Lost Park Campground and dips into a thicket of yellow willows. After 0.2 mile, stay left at the junction with the Brookside-McCurdy Trail and register your party at the free trail register before entering the wilderness area. Follow the trail east as it bends into a stand of shady pines next to Lost Creek. You'll find rock walls in the trees and some nice campsites and fishing pools after 0.5 mile. Continue down a brief rocky section and through an old fence into the open expanse of East Lost Park. Watch for moose thrashing about in the meadows.

The wide expanse you're hiking through is the Lost Park. Willows surround the creek and create a beautiful color show in this high meadow.

Fall color across the valley with aspens above and grasses below.

Mile 2 brings you to more secluded campsites (though, if you camp, take care to ensure you are camped at least 200 feet from the streams here) before depositing you out into the meadow once again. At mile 3.25, you'll find a scenic place to eat lunch on top of a rock overlooking the massive flat park you've been courting all morning. Here you will also find the junction with an unmaintained trail heading southeast up the adjacent drainage. Continue on the trail you came on as it bends northeast, hugging a hillside on the edge of the park until finishing at the gentle saddle after a series of switchbacks. Turn around and return the way you came.

I rated this hike "easy to moderate" because of the Wigwam Trail's flat, well-graded surface, making it ideal for anyone with knee or ankle problems, and it delivers a beautiful sampling of the Lost Creek Wilderness's rounded granite domes without having to negotiate its sometimes-challenging elevation gains. Hikers can turn back any time before the full 5.25-mile length to make this easy-to-moderate hike a mellow stroll through the high meadows of the western section of the wilderness area. The trail can be made as difficult as desired by hiking a longer length on this trail that dives deeper into the wilderness.

Bring plenty of sunscreen on this trail. Despite being below tree line, this trail is largely in the middle of a wide meadow full of sunshine. On a particularly wet and warm year, if you're hiking before the first deep freeze, the marshy park makes it possible to run into some mosquitos. Hence, consider some bug spray in your bag along with the sunscreen. I also have seen moose on this trail, so be alert for them crashing about in the willows by the creek. The long, rumbling road into the Lost Park Trailhead has a lot of fantastic dispersed camping, both on the main road and the Forest Service roads branching off to the south.

THE WIGWAM TRAIL—LOST PARK TRAILHEAD

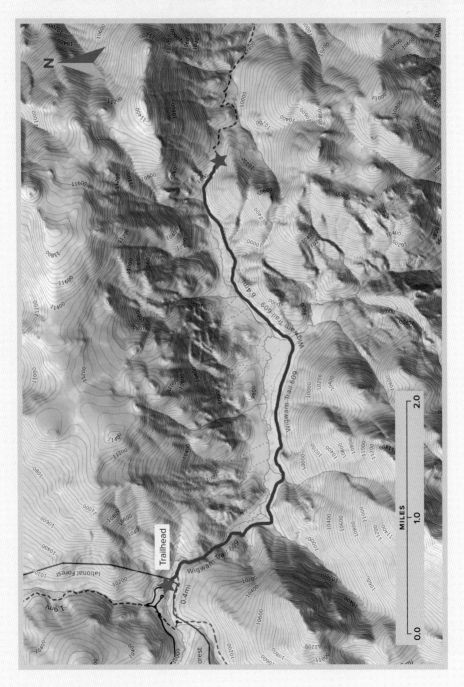

McCULLOUGH GULCH

8

Rating	Difficult
Round-Trip Distance	7.25 miles
Elevation Gain	1,500 feet
Round-Trip Time	7 hours
Maps	Trails Illustrated 109: Breckenridge, Tennessee Pass
Main Attraction	Tundra color, waterfalls, mining ruins, alpine majesty

COMMENT: A beautiful hike in the shadow of Quandary Peak's north face, this hike climbs up the forested drainage to a beautiful lake.

GETTING THERE: From the town of Breckenridge, drive south on Colorado Highway 9 for roughly 9 miles. Just before the road begins to climb into the

Quandary Peak towers over McCullough Gulch.

switchbacks, turn right onto Blue Lakes Road. Immediately after turning onto Blue Lakes Road, the McCullough Gulch shuttle parking area is on your right. Follow all posted parking restrictions.

During the summer months, there is a shuttle that leaves from this parking area to take hikers to the 14er trailhead and to the Upper McCullough Gulch Trailhead. However, in the fall, the shuttle is usually done running. That means you get to hike from the bottom parking area! Don't worry, the road is a beautiful hike in and of itself.

TRAILHEAD: The McCullough Gulch parking area has room for plenty of cars for off-season fall hikers. Park at the lower trailhead and be prepared to climb up the shuttle route for 1.7 miles to the gated

Quandary Peak above the lake with willows and twisted trees right at tree line.

upper part of the road. The county enforces a strict no-parking policy on the road above this parking area.

THE ROUTE: From the lower McCullough Gulch parking area just off CO 9, hike up County Road 851 for 1.7 miles. The road portion of the hike climbs through dense golden aspen groves on a mild grade. The climb levels out and then descends a little bit at 1.1 miles.

At 1.7 miles, the road forks. Stay left to proceed to the upper gate on the road and continue hiking a flat section of road to the start of the off-road hiking trail at 2.25 miles.

The trail climbs a loose alpine rock trail, across a bridge, and up toward the ruins of an old mining claim. Respect the old cabin, as well as the railroad tracks leading out of an old mine.

The trail climbs away from the mining area, though social trails and the often ill-defined trails are marked by cairns. The trail climbs a short series of wooden

The cascades below the lake are multi-layered and beautiful. Photo by Mario Rangel

stairs before crossing alpine scree. The trail can be difficult to follow here, but continue climbing, looking for piles of stones or small brown Forest Service signs that mark the trail with an arrow.

At 3.4 miles from the lower parking area, cross a small rotten-log bridge before reaching a view of White Falls—a waterfall cascading down from the lake through blazing-yellow willows—and enjoying the fall air.

Continue to climb 300 vertical feet through steep rock, scrambling up a hard-to-follow trail. If you find yourself getting into terrain you are uncomfortable with, stop, turn around, and look at the area you just came from.

It is easy to overlook a more established route as you are determined to put one foot in front of the other. The "correct" route on this trail should not put you in danger. Be careful not to get off route, take your time, and be conservative. Use your map.

At 3.7 miles, the trail crests at the beautiful lake. Picturesque in its own right, the lake view is dominated by 14,271-foot Quandary Peak towering over the lake. Quandary is the most climbed 14er in Colorado (thus, the need for a hiker shuttle and a strict parking ban) and is the highest peak in the Tenmile Range.

The lakeside is flush with yellow willows and twisted krummholz pines. "Krummholz" is the German word for twisted wood and has come to be identified with the tortured trees trying to eek out an existence at the very top of the tree line in some of the harshest alpine environs.

Return the way you came, down the trail and to the parking area. I rated this hike "difficult" because of the need to hike from the very bottom of the road. The trail is also ill defined in spots, climbs over 1,000 feet, and has loose rock in some places. It is possible to proceed to the upper lake, but be confident in your route-finding skills and stamina.

THERE IS AN OPTION TO CAMP at the bottom of the spur road that branches to the right off the main road climbing along the beginning of this hike. Down Forest Road 851, there are a number of incredible dispersed campsites. The road down to these will pose a slight challenge for a passenger car and may best be left for higher-clearance vehicles. However, camping at one of these sites allows you to park a little closer to the start of the trail.

McCULLOUGH GULCH

COLORADO'S BEST HIKES FOR FALL COLORS

CAHILL POND— MUELLER STATE PARK

Rating	Moderate
Round-Trip Distance	2.8 miles
Elevation Gain	400 feet
Round-Trip Time	2.5 hours
Maps	Trails Illustrated 137: Pikes Peak, Cañon City; State Park paper maps are available at the trailhead
Main Attraction	A sprawling state park with plenty of aspens and peak views, just forty-five minutes from Colorado Springs

COMMENT: An excellent meandering hike through different forests, grasslands, and riparian ecosystems with views of grand peaks beyond . . . all within an hour of Colorado Springs. No dogs are allowed on this hike!

Sentinel Point towers above the hike.

This hike has wide-open meadows with long views.

GETTING THERE: From Colorado Springs, drive west on US 24 toward Woodland Park. Pass through Woodland Park and drive US 24 to the town of Divide. Drive south on Colorado 67 for 4 miles to the Mueller State Park entrance. Turn west into the park, pay the state park entrance fee, and drive to the end of the park road (roughly 3 miles). The trailhead is at the end of the Turley Meadow Campground at the very end of the state park road system.

TRAILHEAD: The Grouse Mountain Trailhead is at the end of the state park road. There is plenty of parking, and restrooms are available in the campground. Note that hikers do have to have a State Parks pass, be it a day pass or a season pass. Again, note that no dogs are allowed on this hike.

THE ROUTE: One note before we begin: Mueller State Park does not name their trails. Rather, they are numbered. This can get confusing. Take a photo of the map at the trailhead or grab a park map before you start hiking.

From the trailhead, hike north through an open meadow with aspens and pines. Stay right on the Trail 17 then straight on 17e. There are a lot of confusing trails here, but you want to stay southward on Trail 17. At 0.5 mile, keep going straight on 17.

The trail junctions become less confusing here, and the views open to the peaks above, primarily Pikes Peak and Sentinel Point. The trail descends into an aspen forest. At 1 mile, turn left onto Trail 36 and take in the view of a colorful hillside panorama.

Follow the trail as it turns inward to a dense aspen grove and hike through a mixed forest to the bottom of an open meadow at 1.5 miles. The aspen trees here are heavily scarred on the trunks up to about 8 feet in height. The black scars are old marks from where elk ate the aspen bark. New scars can show fresh wood on the aspen trunks.

Turn left (west) onto Trail 34 and proceed through a beautiful open meadow ringed with aspens and hoisted high with colorful grasses below. The trail climbs slowly through yellow and red sideoats grama and bluestem grasses and passes the Cahill Pond to the south. While the pond may be more of a marsh at this time of year, the aspen color around the moisture is bright and gorgeous.

The Cahill Pond was named for the Cahill homestead and formed by springs and rain runoff. Water was used for cattle on the state park's namesake Mueller Ranch. Today, the pond and surrounding meadow make for great habitat for all types of high-alpine meadow wildlife.

The trail skirts the edge between the meadow and the aspen forest.

Cahill Pond.

Climb out of the meadow and into a mixed forest on a gravel-covered trail, eventually moving onto a wider gravel trail. At 2.1 miles, stay straight on Trail 34 to keep climbing out of the meadow and toward the Cahill cabin ruins and a picnic table. Take a break to enjoy the fall color views down-valley and of peaks above.

Continue hiking uphill to 2.25 miles and stay south as the trail continues to climb. Keep going up to 2.5 miles and turn right, back toward the trailhead. Follow the signage to return to the trailhead parking area.

CAHILL POND—MUELLER STATE PARK

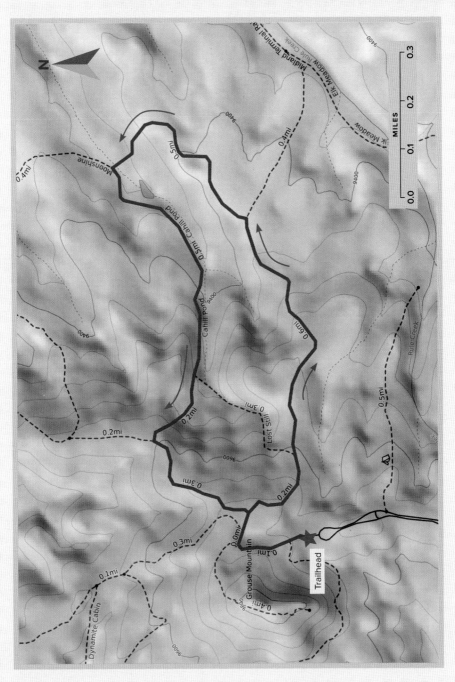

RACCOON TRAIL— GOLDEN GATE CANYON STATE PARK

10

Rating	Moderate
Round-Trip Distance	2.6 miles
Elevation Gain	486 feet
Round-Trip Time	2 hours
Maps	Trails Illustrated 100: Golden, Boulder
Main Attraction	A moderate hike through dense aspens with views of the Continental Divide

The aspens hug the trail as it winds underneath a dramatic cliff face.

COMMENT: Golden Gate Canyon State Park is close to Denver but feels a million miles away. Immaculate campgrounds and well-marked trails like this one make the trip well worth it.

GETTING THERE: From Denver, take US 6 west to the town of Golden. At the mouth of Clear Creek Canyon, continue straight (north) onto Colorado Highway 93. Proceed 1.4 miles, turn left (west) on Golden Gate Canyon Road, and continue 14 miles until turning right onto Mountain Base Road. Continue for 3.2 miles and turn right onto Gap Road. In 0.5 mile, Panorama Point is on your left (the north side of the road).

TRAILHEAD: The Panorama Point Trailhead is a very popular trailhead and vista point in the park. Arrive early to snag a parking spot as it is quite competitive. The trailhead has an outhouse and observation deck.

On the climb back to the trailhead, the trail becomes rocky and steep.

THE ROUTE: From the overlook boardwalk at the Panorama Point Trailhead, take the short stairs down to the dirt trail descending west from the deck.

Note that this is a loop trail. I hiked the loop clockwise and wrote these descriptions as such. I'll explain why I think that's the better option in the trail instructions below.

The first section of trail gently descends immediately and continuously, switch-backing through a mixed-species forest, and is predominantly a fine-crushed gravel surface with some protruding roots. At 0.65 mile, turn right to continue along the Raccoon Trail.

From here, the trail continues its constant downhill attitude but along a sandy, uniform surface. At 1.1 miles, the trail has a junction and the option to connect to the Reverend's Ridge Campground. Stay straight on the trail you came from to continue on the Raccoon Loop.

The bottom point of the hike comes at 1.2 miles. Take a break because the flat part does not last long before climbing steadily. Here the trail offers views of the majestic rocky ridge above, and the aspen colors begin to get more saturated.

Raccoon Trail—Golden Gate Canyon State Park

Climb through a section of steep, loose rock. This section of loose footing is the main reason why I recommend hiking clockwise. I find it much easier to climb loose rock than to descend it. Another advantage to hiking clockwise is that hikers are rewarded with more present views of the ridge above the trail.

At 2.1 miles, stay right at the Mule Deer junction and continue climbing. The final push of trail is a golden tunnel of leaves under young aspens. Return to the east side of the parking lot at 2.5 miles and admire the panorama of peaks looking north. There is a diagram on the overlook deck that shows which peaks are visible, but North Arapaho Peak and Apache Peak are some of the more prominent high peaks.

This is a fantastic trail in a refreshing state park close to Denver. The trail and the park as a whole offer consistent dense aspen stands alight with color, and the conifer forests are thick and healthy, largely free of the beetle kill plaguing the forests farther to the west. Because this is a state park, all visitors must either purchase a day pass ($10 at the time of writing) or an annual pass.

I rated this hike "moderate" because of the middling length and elevation gain. While the trail descends and climbs without a rest, the grades are manageable and the scenery is enjoyable at every point. The trail surface is fantastic, save for the loose rock on the steep incline on the way back.

Panorama point.

RACCOON TRAIL—GOLDEN GATE CANYON STATE PARK

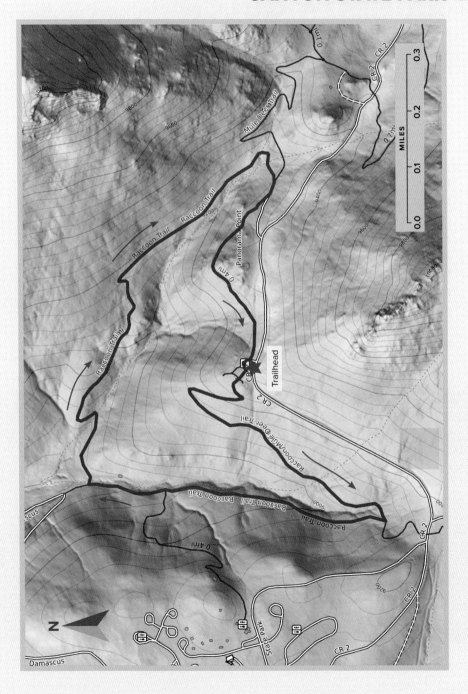

RAINBOW GULCH

11

Rating	Easy
Round-Trip Distance	1.2 miles
Elevation Gain	250 feet
Round-Trip Time	1 hour
Maps	Trails Illustrated 137: Pikes Peak, Cañon City
Main Attraction	An easy hike to a scenic reservoir, close to the major Front Range cities

COMMENT: A rainbow of colors on a flat hike along the inlet stream for the Rampart Range Reservoir, this hike is a fun day hike near Colorado Springs.

GETTING THERE: From Colorado Springs, drive west on US Highway 24 toward Woodland Park. Just before entering Woodland Park, turn right (north) onto County Road 22 (Rampart Range Road). After 2.4 miles, turn right onto Loy Creek Road. Follow Loy Creek Road for 1.5 miles before turning right onto Rampart Range Road

Left: The south side of the reservoir winds through beautiful aspens. **Right:** Rampart Reservoir in a low-water year.

The grasses below the aspens are beautiful in and of themselves.

again. Follow Rampart Range Road for 2.3 miles until arriving at the trailhead on the east side of the road.

TRAILHEAD: The Rainbow Gulch Trailhead is on the east side of the well-maintained, dirt Rampart Range Road. There is ample parking and some signage about the trail and the area.

THE ROUTE: From the Rainbow Gulch Trailhead, hike east under a tall ponderosa pine forest. The trail is wide and well maintained as it meanders toward the reservoir. The trail winds peacefully through occasional colorful aspen groves and pine trees.

At 0.75 mile, the trail crosses the creek. Stay straight to continue on the trail before crossing another bridge to the more established trail north of the creek. The trail descends gently on the way in. The creek itself is often hard to see beneath a thick cover of colorful willows and aspens. Even the grasses underfoot are alight with color in fall.

At 1.5 miles, a bridge carries hikers to the south side of the reservoir where the trail becomes less established. At this point, hikers can take the trail across the bridge and along the south shores of the reservoir or stay on the north side. The south side winds in and out of an aspen forest in a more shaded route, while the north side follows the bare shore of the lake.

On the south side of the reservoir, there are numerous social trail options, but all skirt the shore of the reservoir. At 1.75 miles, there are good overlooks of the reservoir and surrounding area. This serves as the turnaround point for this write-up. Whichever route along the lakeshore you choose, you can, however, continue as far as you would like. If you're interested in a longer day, the full trek around the reservoir from the bridge on the western tip of the lake comes in at around 11 miles with just shy of 1,000 feet of elevation gain and loss.

I rated this hike easy for its solid footing, modest elevation gain, and short length. The hike is a great option for families and to take your sea-level-dwelling friends and family on when they're in town.

This is also a really nice hike for a beach day, so to speak. Pack a lunch and take a picnic to the lakeshore. Cast a line, take in the views, or push your limits and hike the full loop around the water. Also note that this area is popular with mountain bikers. Be careful on the trail. Keep your ears and eyes open for cyclists and avoid a collision.

The Rampart Range Reservoir fluctuates in water level year to year. It provides the drinking water for Colorado Springs and has the capacity to hold thirteen billion gallons of water. The dam for the reservoir was completed in 1969. The reservoir is known for its water-recreation opportunities near Colorado Springs, including fishing for trout and kokanee salmon.

Walking through dense willows on the edge of the creek.

RAINBOW GULCH

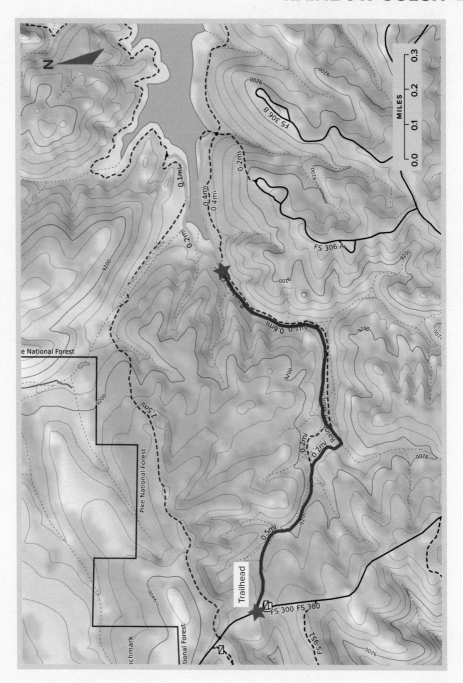

ROYAL ARCH

Rating	Difficult
Round-Trip Distance	3.6 miles
Elevation Gain	1,377 feet
Round-Trip Time	2.5 hours
Maps	Trails Illustrated 100: Boulder, Golden
Main Attraction	A challenging hike with fantastic views from the top

COMMENT: This challenging hike is fantastic in the fall, when temperatures are more mild and a variety of tree species put on a colorful autumn show. This is a Stair-Master of a hike, so prepare your footwear and refine your expectations. This low-elevation hike tends to change colors much later than the peaks in the high country.

Ash trees give the lower parts of the hike a pop of color.

GETTING THERE: In Boulder, this popular urban trailhead is located in the southwest part of town at the intersection of Baseline Road and Ninth Street. From downtown Boulder, drive west on Arapahoe Avenue until meeting Ninth Street. Turn left (south) and proceed to the park.

TRAILHEAD: The Chautauqua Park parking area is a small, busy lot. Get there early to get a spot. Depending on the day of the week and the time of the year, there are fees to park in the lot. Find the meter and pay, if necessary.

THE ROUTE: From the southwest corner of the parking area, by the ranger station, hike up the short stairs to the wide gravel trail and turn left (south). The trail climbs almost immediately as you hike next to the backyards of the Chautauqua cabins.

Starting up the very steep and rocky upper reaches of the trail.

The Colorado Chautauqua was established in 1898. The Chautauqua movement started in New York in 1876 as an educational idea that centered around communal summer learning and recreation. Summer residents enjoyed guest speakers, climbing, horseback riding, and communal living at the base of the Flatirons. Designated a National Historic Landmark in 2006, this is one of the only continuously operating Chautauqua communities in America.

As you climb the popular gravel trail, the diversity of tree species changing colors below the majestic Flatirons is impressive. Brilliant-yellow ash trees change color early, followed by native plum trees, honey locusts, and even the stray walnut tree. Shortgrass prairie foothills grasses turn a brilliant red and yellow as the season continues.

Continue up the wide, busy gravel trail to the restrooms at 0.6 mile, stay right, and then immediately turn left at the Bluebird Shelter sign. Enter a ponderosa pine forest before meeting the Royal Arch signed junction at 0.75 mile. Turn left (west) and continue up the trail as it transforms from a wide, crushed-stone urban path to a steep, root-and-rock filled mountain path. There are two boardwalks, but from here on out, the trail is steep, rocky, and rugged.

Royal Arch.

Stay left at the small junction at 1 mile and cross a dark, narrow canyon full of my favorite Colorado native tree, the box elder, turning yellow and inviting you farther up the canyon to a stone staircase through a scree field. Catch your breath and enjoy views of rock climbers high on the Second Flatiron above and the colorful urban forest in Boulder below.

Continue to climb very steep rocks until reaching the saddle at 1.7 miles. The respite is short-lived but take a moment before descending the very steep wooden stairs about 75 vertical feet. Stay right toward the fencing near the bottom of the descent, bottom out, and then climb again, this time even steeper than before. Finally, at 1.8 miles, the arch comes into view after climbing yet another stone staircase. Enjoy the long views over town from below the majestic arch; then continue back the way you came.

I rated this hike "difficult" because of its relentlessly steep climb on rough terrain. Note that this hike is also very busy. Be prepared for crowds. Start before 8:00 a.m. to avoid the rush. This hike can also be very hot, another reason to start early. Also, check the city website before leaving the house as this trail is often closed for wildlife habitat protection or restoration.

ROYAL ARCH

OLD DILLON RESERVOIR

13

Rating	Easy
Round-Trip Distance	1.5 miles
Elevation Gain	200 feet
Round-Trip Time	1 hour
Maps	Trails Illustrated 149: Eagles Nest and Holy Cross Wilderness
Main Attraction	An easy hike with a lake and panoramic views of the entire Dillon-Silverthorne panorama of fall color

COMMENT: Stuck in I-70 traffic on your way to or from other hikes? Strange! This is a great easy hike to get a nice view of both sides of the Dillon dam. The colorful prelude to ski season can be witnessed by those of all skill levels.

GETTING THERE: From the Silverthorne exit off of I-70, drive east on US Highway 6 to Dillon Dam Road. Turn south onto the Dam Road, proceed through the traffic circle, and drive for 0.7 mile to the Old Dillon Reservoir Trailhead on the north side of the Dam Road.

Look for moose in this area! They sometimes make an appearance.

Looking back down over the larger Dillon Reservoir.

TRAILHEAD: The Old Dillon Reservoir Trailhead is a medium-sized dirt parking lot off the Dillon Dam Road. This is a busy area. Be courteous and park close to other vehicles in order to maximize parking spots.

THE ROUTE: From the parking area, the trail climbs a wide, well-trodden dirt path up the hillside. Switchbacking through aspens and pines, the trail is a gentle climb even here at its most aggressive incline. The trail levels out after the initial switchbacks.

Periodically, the trail opens to views to the south. Just before reaching the upper reservoir, there are fantastic views of the lower Dillon Reservoir.

After 0.4 mile of gentle climbing, you will reach the top of the incline and glimpse the upper lake before descending swiftly onto a wide, gravel path circling the lake.

The lake is a fantastic place to view moose. In fact, on our hike, we met descending parties who had seen a cow moose splashing about in the upper reservoir. Alas, we had no such luck. While wildlife may seem domesticated or docile

The views north from the old reservoir show the beauty of these hills in fall. Photo by Mario Rangel

in an environment such as this where they see a lot of people, never approach or allow dogs to get entangled with moose. Respect wild animals by giving them a wide berth.

Walk around the lake and enjoy each aspect filled with views of hillsides lit up with aspens. To the northwest is the domed Buffalo Mountain with lucky households descending the slopes amid a dense canopy of color. Also spy the Eagles Nest Wilderness and the Gore Range. Across the northern valley are the Byers Peaks and their similar visual display.

To the south, enjoy the view toward Breckenridge, the Tenmile Range, Lake Dillon, and the numerous lakeside campgrounds.

Complete the lakeside loop and rejoin the trail to the parking lot at 1.1 miles. Descend the way you came and end up back at your car at 1.5 miles.

OLD DILLON RESERVOIR

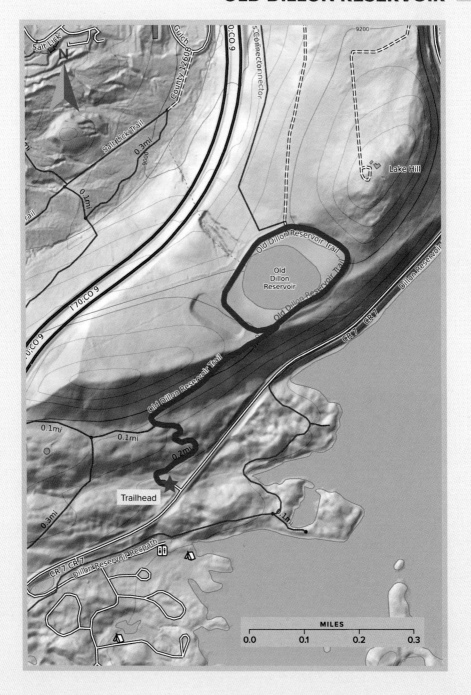

UPPER PINEY RIVER TRAIL— KNEEKNOCKER PASS

14

Rating	Moderate to the cascades, difficult to Kneeknocker Pass
Round-Trip Distance	6 miles to the falls, 7.5 miles to the pass
Elevation Gain	700 feet to the falls, 2,700 feet to Kneeknocker Pass
Round-Trip Time	5–8 hours
Maps	Trails Illustrated 149: Eagles Nest and Holy Cross Wilderness
Main Attraction	Aspen-filled valleys and an alpine amphitheater

COMMENT: An easy, wildlife-filled hike through aspens to a waterfall. Past the falls, a challenging off-trail scramble leads to a beautiful alpine basin.

GETTING THERE: From Vail, head north on Red Sandstone Road for 0.7 mile before turning left onto the dirt road branching off from the apex of one of the road's paved switchbacks. Look for the signs directing you to Piney River Ranch. Drive the

Carrying a heavy load on an alpine trip to Kneeknocker Pass.

The alpine park below Kneeknocker Pass.

dirt road up for 2.7 miles, then stay left on Piney Lake Road, and drive another 4 miles before staying straight onto Piney River Road. Follow signs for the Piney River Ranch. The parking area for the Upper Piney Lake Trail sits just outside of the private resort parking. Park at the Forest Service trailhead to avoid any fees.

TRAILHEAD: The Upper Piney Lake Trailhead sits just outside of the private resort parking. The trail starts to the north of the road.

THE ROUTE: Cross the road from the parking area and stay on the trail as it skirts around the private ranch. The trail gradually climbs up the Piney River Valley, over-looking majestic Piney Lake. Sign in to the Eagles Nest Wilderness area at 0.5 mile and begin to climb away from the lake. The willows along the river light up yellow, and the aspens on the slope above make this an excellent, colorful, easy hike close to Denver. Mount Powell and the ridgeline above the valley frame your climb into the aspen forest for the next 2.5 miles. The trail steepens as you near the cascades, weaving in and out of aspen and pine stands. At 3 miles, the trail reaches a pleasant cascade, a perfect place for lunch and your turn-back point if you were here for a moderate hike.

Moose are extremely common in this area. Use caution when admiring them from a distance. Moose were only occasional visitors to Colorado as recently as the 1970s. In 1978, the occasional moose wandering south from the more northern parts of the Rockies got a boost when Colorado Parks and Wildlife (CPW) introduced twelve moose from Utah into North Park, near Wyoming in the far north of the

Entering the meadow below the pass.

state. CPW continued relocating moose from other parts of the country into the northern reaches of Colorado. Since then, the moose population has grown considerably into a self-sustaining, thriving population of nearly three thousand across the state. Moose are most commonly seen in the area around the small town of Walden and the larger North Park area, but the dense thickets of trees and abundant water (willows are their favorite food) on this trail give you a great chance of seeing one of these massive creatures. Moose can weigh up to 1,200 pounds, with bulls standing up to 6 feet tall at the shoulders. Give them a wide berth if you are fortunate enough to spot one.

I rated this hike "moderate" because of the middling distance and the sometimes-uneven footing. This is a popular trail through forested areas filled with roots and shallow creek crossings. If you choose to tackle the sidebar hike accompanying the main description, the rating is a hearty "difficult" as routefinding skills come into play and a significant elevation gain greets hikers.

ADVANCED HIKERS WITH SOLID ROUTEFINDING SKILLS can use a map and compass to ascend to Kneeknocker Pass, an informally named, unmarked pass that gives views down into the east side of the wilderness area. Cairns occasionally mark the informal route as you climb the side drainage away from the river. But a map and compass will be your true guides here. Continue to climb the social trail, steeply upward, for 0.75 mile before entering a majestic alpine basin below the pass. Mountain goats roam among the crags and the fiery red undergrowth. The pass is located at roughly N39° 45.120' / W106° 20.416' if you want to climb for the views overlooking the east side of the wilderness and its many difficult-to-access lakes. Return the way you came.

UPPER PINEY RIVER TRAIL—
KNEEKNOCKER PASS

NORTHERN MOUNTAINS

Coyote Valley: This is the headwaters of the mighty, and all-important, Colorado River (Hike 19).

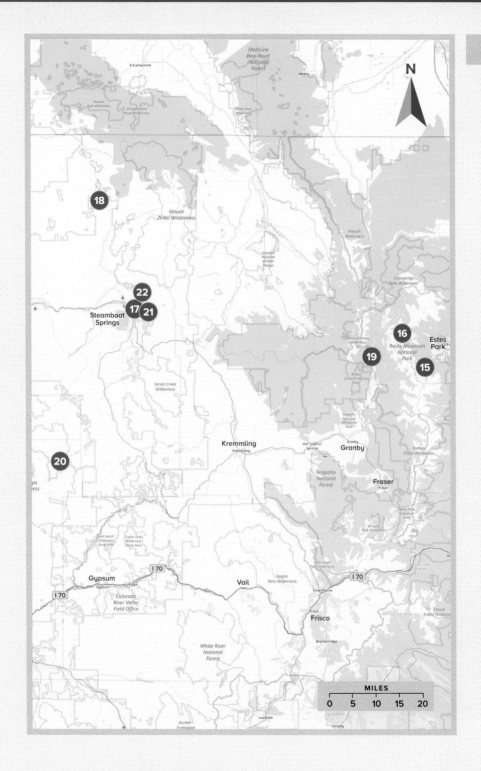

GLACIER GORGE

15

Rating	Difficult
Round-Trip Distance	11.5 miles
Elevation Gain	2,600 feet
Round-Trip Time	8 hours
Maps	Trails Illustrated 200: Rocky Mountain National Park
Main Attraction	Alpine tundra fall splendor

COMMENT: One of the best spots in the backcountry of Colorado's most well-known national park, this challenging hike has it all.

GETTING THERE: From Estes Park, drive west on US Highway 36 toward the Rocky Mountain National Park Beaver Meadows Entrance Station. Pay the park entrance fee and turn south (left) onto Bear Lake Road. Continue down the road for 8.3 miles to the Glacier Gorge Trailhead on the south (left) side of the road.

A hillside of aspens.

TRAILHEAD: The Glacier Gorge Trailhead is small and crowded. Pay attention to road signs that indicate rules for parking at the lots on the ever-popular Bear Lake Road. The overwhelming likelihood is that you will have to park down-valley at the park-and-ride. The National Park Service operates easy-to-use, timely shuttle busses to take hikers to the popular trailheads at the end of the road.

THE ROUTE: From the Glacier Gorge shuttle bus stop and parking area, hike west for a third of a mile. The trail can be a bit confusing here as this is a busy intersection of multiple trails. Look for rangers, usually stationed nearby, and ask questions if you're confused. Turn south (left) to hike toward Alberta Falls.

Keyboard of the Winds above high-alpine bushes.

The trail climbs very gradually until reaching Alberta Falls after 0.8 mile. Alberta Falls is a picturesque thirty-foot falls that can get crowded since they are about a mile from the trailhead and only 200 feet above the parking lot. Take some pictures and then move on away from the crowds. You have even more beautiful sights ahead of you.

Follow the most well-established and heavily trafficked trail uphill after the falls. There are a couple of climbers' trails and fire crew trails in this area that you don't want to be on. The trail continues above the falls, undulating back and forth and climbing gently up the hillside before reaching the junction with the North Longs Peak Trail at 1.5 miles. Stay to the right, heading westward and progressing on a level trail. At 2 miles, you will reach the junction of a diverse set of trails. Instead of heading up to the Loch or Lake Haiyaha, turn left to continue to Glacier Gorge.

After making the turn, the trail proceeds through some flat marshy areas near Mills Lake. There are wooden boardwalks, and at this point, the crowds have hopefully begun to clear out for you. At 3.3 miles, pass the junction for the Glacier Gorge backcountry site. This is a fantastic place to spend the night *if* you had the patience, forethought, and luck to snag a permit the moment the backcountry office began accepting reservations in the spring.

Left: McHenry's Peak above Black Lake. **Right:** Alpine color above Black Lake.

From here, the trail begins to climb at a much steeper clip, often incorporating wooden steps built into the trail on the steeper sections, as you climb toward Black Lake. Emerge onto the shores of majestic Black Lake at 4.6 miles. The peak rising to the west of the lake is the Arrowhead, while McHenrys Peak rises to the southwest. Both are coveted summits for technical climbers in the park.

Up to this point, the hike has featured abundant glimpses of aspens on the nearby hillside. To really understand why this hike makes it into this book as a fall color hike, proceed to the east of Black Lake. From here, the trail grows less maintained and steeper as it climbs above tree line into the alpine. Continue on the trail up into the amphitheater above.

Reach Frozen Lake at 5.75 miles and 11,600 feet. This is one of the most incredible views in Rocky Mountain National Park. The pointed monolith to your east is the spearhead, north of Chiefs Head Peak. Farther east in the same amphitheater is the dramatic, jagged Keyboard of the Winds on the rugged western slopes of mighty Longs Peak. Return the way you came. Throughout the entire alpine environment, the alpine tundra plants are ablaze with red, yellow, and orange.

I rated this hike "difficult" because of its length, elevation gain, and rocky footing. This is a long hike into the heart of Rocky Mountain's wilderness. Carry plenty of sunscreen for the alpine environment. Stay on the trail through the fragile tundra.

GLACIER GORGE

Trailhead

TUNDRA COMMUNITIES TRAIL

16

Rating	Easy
Round-Trip Distance	1.2 miles
Elevation Gain	300 feet
Round-Trip Time	1 hour
Maps	Trails Illustrated 200: Rocky Mountain National Park
Main Attraction	Tundra plants, alpine views of the Gorge Lakes

COMMENT: An easy trek high above tree line amid the fall tundra colors, accessed by one of the most iconic drives on earth.

Looking south over the Arrowhead Lakes basin.

GETTING THERE: From Estes Park, head west out of town into the National Park on US Highway 36. Pay your park entrance fee at the Beaver Meadows Entrance and follow the signs toward Trail Ridge Road. Stay straight at the Deer Ridge junction to transition onto US 34 and begin your climb up to the tundra on Trail Ridge Road. Follow the road for 13 miles, passing through Rock Cut, to the trailhead parking on the north side of the road.

TRAILHEAD: The Tundra Communities Trailhead is a busy roadside trailhead at the Rock Cut landmark with two bathrooms and limited parking. Be careful driving and walking here.

The scenic tundra with 100-mile views.

THE ROUTE: Leave the bathroom area and climb the paved trail on the north side of the road. Interpretive signs point out the various plant life that have adapted to life in the clouds and above the trees. Many of these grasses turn a brilliant red during the fall. At 0.34 mile, turn onto the Mushroom Rocks spur overlook for views of Haynach and the Gorge Lakes.

Mushroom Rocks are three appropriately named mushroom-shaped landmarks in the middle of the hike that are worth exploring. The top of the rocks is schist, a kind of rock here formed by sand, clay, and silt that rested at the bottom of an ancient ocean. Granite from volcanic activity makes up the "stems" of the mushrooms and is a paler shade. The granite eroded faster than the schist and formed the distinctive mushroom stems.

The trail becomes more level after Mushroom Rocks, gradually climbing to the overlook at the end of the trail at 0.6 mile.

Scramble on the rocks at your own risk to reach a metal plaque naming the peaks surrounding you in 360 degrees. The views of the aspen forests far below and the pristine tundra immediately around you are a sight to behold.

The alpine tundra is a land of extremes year-round. From heavy snows to fierce lightning storms, the weather is volatile this high up. The fall season brings a unique set of colors as grasses, forbs, and the occasional shrub turn varying colors

Top: Approaching Mushroom Rocks. **Bottom:** Looking back down toward Trail Ridge Road.

COLORADO'S BEST HIKES FOR FALL COLORS

of orange, red, brown, and yellow. One particularly beautiful plant is the alpine bearberry with its brilliant copper leaves. Another to look out for is the alpine avens, which flowers throughout June but then transforms its leaves from green to bright red in August.

I rated this hike "easy" because of its short distance and modest elevation gain. The walking surface is also partially paved and easy. Some people, however, have a very hard time being at such high elevations. Even with extended acclimation times, some find the thin air gives them a myriad of health problems. Check in with your group often, especially if any of them are visiting the alpine from the lower parts of the country. You are well above tree line on this hike, and as such, bring plenty of sunscreen, a hat, and sunglasses.

The panoramic peak-finding plaque at the top of the hike.

The drive along Trail Ridge Road is indescribably beautiful. But the road is one of the highest in America and is closed for much of the year. That means that this area is prone to sudden extreme weather. On a road with no guardrails for much of the drive, this can be a dangerous situation. The National Park Service does a fantastic job of maintaining the road and closing it when necessary, but assess if you are up for the drive. And don't let the driver's eyes wander to the incredible views around every curve. Pay attention to the road and save the "oooohs" and "ahhhs" for the hike!

TUNDRA COMMUNITIES TRAIL

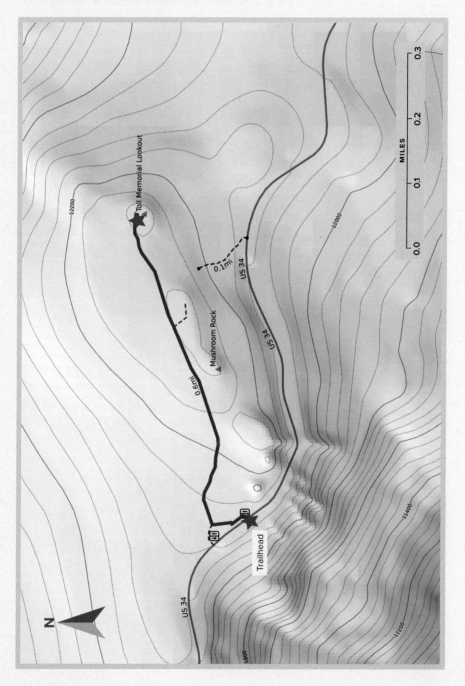

Toll Memorial Lookout

0.1mi

US 34

Mushroom Rock

0.6mi

US 34

Trailhead

US 34

12200

12000

11400

11200

11800

N

MILES

0.0   0.1   0.2   0.3

SPRING CREEK TRAIL— STEAMBOAT SPRINGS

17

Rating	Easy
Round-Trip Distance	1.6 miles
Elevation Gain	200 feet
Round-Trip Time	1 hour
Maps	Trails Illustrated 118: Steamboat Springs, Rabbit Ears Pass
Main Attraction	Easy, aspen-filled hike right from town

COMMENT: A beautiful, easy hike right outside of town ending at a pair of ponds.

GETTING THERE: From downtown Steamboat Springs, walk or drive northeast on Third Street. Turn right on Maple Street and take Maple until it ends at the trailhead. It is also possible to start your hike from just behind the Steamboat Springs Post Office.

TRAILHEAD: The Spring Creek Trailhead has parking on the sides of the road right before a gate. The parking area is at the corner of Amethyst Drive and Maple Street. As always, for trails leaving from such populated areas, make sure you're not parking illegally or blocking any driveways or loading zones.

THE ROUTE: From the trailhead at Maple and Amethyst, hike east on the Spring Creek Road, which is open to hikers and cyclists but closed to cars. Hike along the road for 0.5 mile. The trail here is interspersed with private property but features a thick understory of willows and oaks along the creek, complete with the occasional riverside bench.

Take a break on one of the scenic creek-side benches.

The second lake on the hike is placid and teeming with wildlife.

At 0.5 mile, you'll find the lower of two ponds. The lower pond has a dog park and plenty of spots to relax and enjoy views of the surrounding willows and aspens. Continue on the upper branch of the trail to the second pond, teaming with musk-rats and ringed with orange and red oaks. Past the second pond, at 0.8 mile is a small bridge that leads the trail into a dense willow and aspen thicket. Social trails abound around the back of the upper pond and up toward private property. Explore as much as you like, then turn back, and return the way you came.

Note that this trail continues for 5 miles, one-way, all the way up to the Dry Lake Trailhead along Buffalo Pass Road. At the top, you can catch the Flash of Gold Trail (Hike 22) to make for a longer day. If you want to explore farther, be prepared for more mountain bike traffic and a steeper climb. Also make sure to check regulations for one-way restrictions on the upper stretches of trail. Although mountain bikes are supposed to yield to hikers as a rule, this is not always the case. Approach bikes cautiously when hiking, especially if there are blind curves or low-visibility areas where a cyclist may not see you until it is too late to avoid an accident. Be smart and courteous.

Left: A small bridge on the far side of the lakes. **Right:** Scrub oak blazing orange.

At the lower pond, as noted, is a dog park. That means hikers should be pre-pared for off-leash dogs, supervised by their owners. If you are hiking with a dog, make sure you are ready to encounter off-leash dogs and plan accordingly. Dogs are required to be on leash for the entirety of this trail, with the exception of the dog park areas.

I rated his hike "easy" as I only hiked it to the upper pond. The mileage is low, and the elevation gain is negligible. The trail is smooth and easy to the upper pond, and even the overgrown, more informal trails leading around the pond are easy to navigate and require little effort to experience the reward of this beautiful, close-to-town hike. If you choose to proceed beyond 2 miles from the lower trailhead in town, the steepness of the trail begins to increase quite a bit.

Start early in the day to avoid hot, sunny sections by the ponds (and farther up the trail, if you choose to proceed). Starting early will also give you a jump on the crowds, as this can be a very popular local excursion. Sunscreen is a must for exposed sections of trail here.

SPRING CREEK TRAIL—STEAMBOAT SPRINGS

TOMBSTONE NATURE TRAIL— STEAMBOAT LAKE

18

Rating	Easy
Round-Trip Distance	1.1 miles
Elevation Gain	150 feet
Round-Trip Time	1 hour
Maps	Trails Illustrated 116: Hahns Peak, Steamboat Lake
Main Attraction	Panoramic views of hillsides full of aspen and red scrub oak

COMMENT: Situated above Steamboat Lake in Steamboat Lake State Park, this is an excellent family hike that gives panoramic views of one of the most colorful but isolated parts of the state.

GETTING THERE: From Steamboat Springs, drive north on County Road 129 for 25 miles. The drive north is absolutely beautiful. Once you enter Hahns Peak Village, a tiny collection of stores and services, turn left immediately after, into the state park. Pay the state park entrance fee ($9 per vehicle at the time of publishing) and proceed past the visitor center to the Tombstone Nature Trail Trailhead, a small parking area to the left.

TRAILHEAD: The Tombstone Nature Trail Trailhead is a small parking area with picnic facilities on the left, before the boat inspection station. Restrooms are available at the visitor center.

THE ROUTE: This loop hike is best done counterclockwise. The hike starts on the northwest side of the parking area and

Aspens ring Tombstone Ridge.

Steamboat Lake from the top of Tombstone Ridge.

meanders through flat meadows with views of the lake. Before climbing the hill ahead of you, the trail takes you closer to the lake where benches offer a view of Hahns Peak to the north. If you look closely, you can see the remains of an old fire lookout tower, completed in 1912.

After 0.25 mile, begin to climb away from the shore into a pine forest. At 0.5 mile, approach a ridge above the shore with views of Sand Mountain and cliffs across the lake. Continue climbing gently above the shore with views of Hahns Peak back to the north, climbing back into pines.

After 0.75 mile, there is a short detour spur trail to the historic site of the Wheeler family graves. The family homesteaded the area in 1921, and the site of the memorial houses the remains of two children. Arriving from Sterling, Colorado, the family experienced a harsh first year with deep snow and a paucity of food. They survived on snowshoe hares, grouse, and dried food preserved for the winters. Rose and James Wheeler lost two children at birth, a daughter named Ruth and a son named Sonny Boy, and they are interred here. Respect the graves as a beautiful resting place and continue back down the spur trail to continue your hike.

Hahns Peak stands tall to the north of Steamboat Lake.

Past the graves, the trail emerges back to lake views and an aspen forest. The trail descends back to the parking and picnic area.

FOR THOSE WISHING TO UNDERTAKE A MORE CHALLENGING HIKE with grandiose panoramas of the colorful hillsides, climbing Hahns Peak is a 3.6-mile, 1,400-foot out-and-back to the top of the peak. From the Tombstone Trail, a small structure is barely visible at the top of Hahns Peak. This is the Hahns Peak fire lookout, finished in 1912. Before cell phones, GPS, and satellite imagery, a national network of fire lookouts was constructed on high peaks to watch for smoke and report fires as they emerged. Fire lookouts were outfitted with advanced maps and scopes to pinpoint where crews needed to respond in order to attack the fire. Decommissioning of the Hahns Peak lookout spanned the 1940s and 1950s and led to the structure falling into disrepair. In 2014, it was listed on Colorado's annual list of most endangered places. The Forest Service and Historic Routt County partnered to restore the structure from 2014 to 2017, and today the site allows visitors to enjoy the view from the restored cabin and engage with educational materials on site about the fascinating history of fire lookouts across the West. The lookout is located at almost 11,000 feet. The trail begins off Forest Service Road 490 north of the village of Hahns Peak. For another hike to a fire lookout, see Hike 4.

TOMBSTONE NATURE TRAIL— STEAMBOAT LAKE

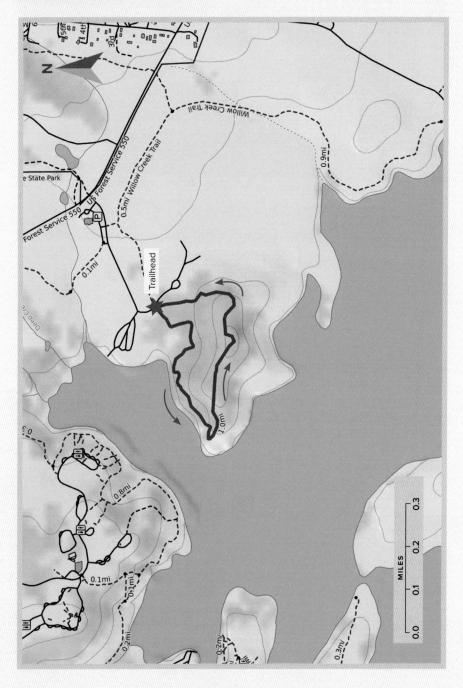

COYOTE VALLEY

19

Rating	Easy
Round-Trip Distance	1.2 miles
Elevation Gain	Negligible
Round-Trip Time	1 hour
Maps	Trails Illustrated 200: Rocky Mountain National Park
Main Attraction	Bugling elk, the headwaters of the Colorado River

COMMENT: The Kawuneeche Valley is renowned for a fall spectacle apart from the colors sweeping the grasslands: bugling elk. The mating songs of elk fill the air at dawn and dusk. This easy trail allows lucky guests to view the spectacle.

GETTING THERE: From Granby, at the junction of US 34 and US 40, drive north on US 34 toward Rocky Mountain National Park. Continue 22 miles, paying the park entrance fee at the Grand Lake Entrance, to the Coyote Valley Trailhead to the west on your left.

Crushed stone trails and big views.

Follow the easy trail through the valley, watching for elk.

TRAILHEAD: The Coyote Valley Trailhead is a small (no vehicles over 18 feet allowed) forested trailhead in the Kawuneeche Valley. The trailhead has restrooms and a small parking area.

THE ROUTE: From the Coyote Valley Trailhead, the trail starts amid a dense old-growth pine forest. Walk over the bridge and stay right on the crushed limestone trail as it follows the fledgling Colorado River. These are its headwaters on its way to the sea. Meadow grasses and sedges, fed by the high water table, grow abundantly here and will have turned shades of yellow and red by September. Views across the valley feature an immense aspen forest on the slopes of Mount Baker.

At the 0.33-mile mark, the trail enters the valley and progresses upstream. At a little over 0.5 mile, the trail turns to dirt and continues to the glacial-valley turn-around point. Social trails continue up valley to scenic vistas if you choose to press on.

This hike is included in this book for its beauty but also because if you arrive at dawn or dusk, you have a good chance of catching one of the Rocky Mountain's greatest fall spectacles: the elk rut. During September and October, male elk put on a courtship display that includes the characteristic trumpeting bugle call. The call starts low in pitch and ends in an almost squeal. The call serves to alert females of the presence of a bull elk looking to mate. Elk are large animals. Give them a wide berth especially this time of year (the National Park Service recommends staying at least 75 feet from elk and other large animals). This hike gives you a chance of catching the annual spectacle, whether by eye or ear, particularly at dawn and dusk.

About halfway up the slopes of Mount Baker, you may notice a horizontal line crossing the mountain. This is the Grand Ditch, an irrigation project that diverts water from the Never Summer Mountains from the Colorado River watershed, across the Continental Divide, and to Long Draw Reservoir and Front Range communities. Completed in 1936, the ditch has consistently drawn criticism from the National Park Service for its measurable withholding of water from the fertile Kawuneeche Valley.

THIS AREA IS RIGHT ON THE EDGE OF THE DEVASTATING 2020 EAST TROUBLESOME FIRE. Most of the meadow on this hike remained untouched, but much of the rest of the valley was not so fortunate. The fire scorched 193,812 acres and ended the 2020 season as the second-largest wildfire in state history (behind the nearby Cameron Peak Fire, which also burned in 2020). The fire began on October 14 and grew exponentially in size over the next ten days, forcing the evacuation of 35,000 people and killing two. Many of the pine trees on the west side of Rocky Mountain National Park had been devastated by beetle kill. These dead trees provided ample fuel for the fire to spread. The fire was not fully contained until November 30, 2020. As our climate changes, fires like this will, unfortunately, become more common and severe. If you must have a campfire, never leave it unattended and make sure to fully extinguish it when you leave.

COYOTE VALLEY

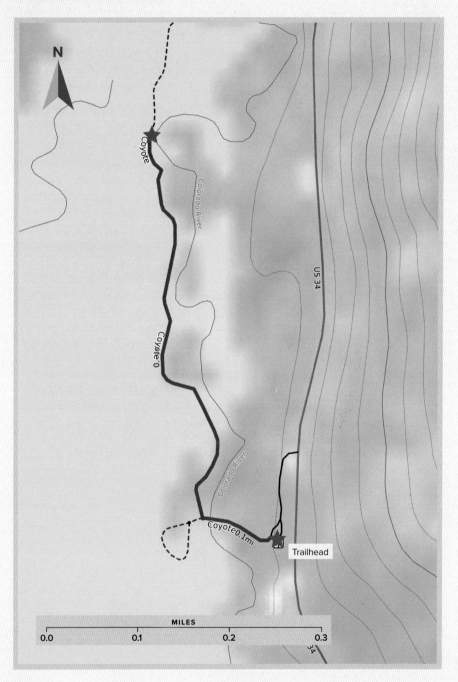

DEVIL'S CAUSEWAY

20

Rating	Difficult
Round-Trip Distance	10.4 miles
Elevation Gain	2,000 feet
Round-Trip Time	5–8 hours
Maps	Trails Illustrated 150: Flat Tops North
Main Attraction	An adventurous hike with panoramic views

COMMENT: A dramatic scramble across a narrow passage on top of stunning cliffs with equally amazing panoramic views of the Flat Tops Wilderness. This hike involves scrambling across a dangerous narrow section of rocks on top of 600-foot sheer cliffs. The trail is as narrow as 3 feet wide and requires great care. Do not undertake this hike lightly.

GETTING THERE: From the small town of Yampa, drive to the southwest corner of town and pick up County Road 7 near the Antlers Café and Bar. Drive south on CR

Crossing one of the scree fields below the causeway.

Tundra plants ablaze with fall color and the Flat Tops above.

7, which transitions to Forest Service Road 900. After roughly 11 miles, stay right to climb the road as it navigates to the top of the Yamcolo Reservoir dam. At the top of the dam, continue westward on FR 900 for another 5.7 miles to Stillwater Reservoir.

TRAILHEAD: Stillwater Reservoir has roadside parking and some signage about the risks of navigating the causeway. The trail starts from the east side of the lake.

THE ROUTE: This loop is best done counterclockwise. From the trailhead, hike west above the lake with sweeping views of aspens and the distinctive Flat Top mountains. At the 0.75-mile mark, stay right on Trail 1119 and sign in to the wilderness register. Climb steadily through a pine forest at the 1-mile mark and enjoy the view above of the centerpiece of your hike: the thrilling Devil's Causeway narrows.

At the 1.6-mile mark, the trail steepens through talus and flaming aspens before crossing above a small alpine lake and entering the alpine tundra around 2 miles into your day. From here, navigate the well-designed switchbacks to a saddle at the 2.6-mile mark. Take a moment to enjoy the sweeping views of the Flat Tops Wilderness spread out around you. After catching your breath, climb the steep slope to the southwest before finally reaching the top of the causeway ridge at 2.8 miles.

From here, take a breath; assess the weather and your group's fitness. Navigating the causeway requires concentration and intentional foot placement. The causeway land bridge is only a couple hundred feet in length but narrows to as few as 3 feet wide with tremendous exposure and 600+ foot cliffs dropping off on each side of the footpath.

The views here are majestic with the tundra full of fall color and aspen-covered hills in the distance. The causeway is thrilling and reminiscent of the most dramatic alpine technical climbs around the state. After carefully navigating the bridge, the hike transitions to a leisurely gradual downhill trek back to the trailhead.

The trail meanders down through low-growth bushes and climbs up into the open tundra. Fall brings an array of yellow and red hues to the alpine tundra. Enjoy the views under foot and above as you meander slowly down. Incredible views of the Chinese Wall formation and the distant mountains to the south and west help pass the time.

At 6.1 miles, stay left on the Stillwater Trail before climbing to a small ridge then following the Bear River Trail signs with views of a colorful valley before you. Continue to descend switchbacks as the landscape gets wetter with alpine tarns and ponds spread throughout the final miles of the hike. At 8 miles, the trail flattens out

Switchbacks below the final causeway approach.

Left: The start of the narrow causeway with sheer drops on both sides. **Right:** After the causeway, the hike crosses tundra with expansive views.

and begins to cross small creeks. The trail crosses in and out of quiet pine forests before leaving the wilderness at just over 9 miles. Meet the trail back to the parking area at 9.6 miles and walk east, back to the reservoir along the same spur of trail that you began your day on.

The Flat Tops Wilderness is the second-largest wilderness area in the state, behind the Weminuche Wilderness in Southwest Colorado. The unique flat-table mountains are made of volcanic basalt and stand in stark contrast to the rounded and jagged mountains across the rest of the state. The area is known for high-quality backpacking, fishing, and wildlife viewing.

I rated this hike "difficult" because of its length, commitment, and dangerous rock passage across the causeway. This hike is certainly not for everyone. If you are not confident hiking on exposed rock with high-stakes consequences in the event of a slip underfoot, don't attempt this hike.

DEVIL'S CAUSEWAY

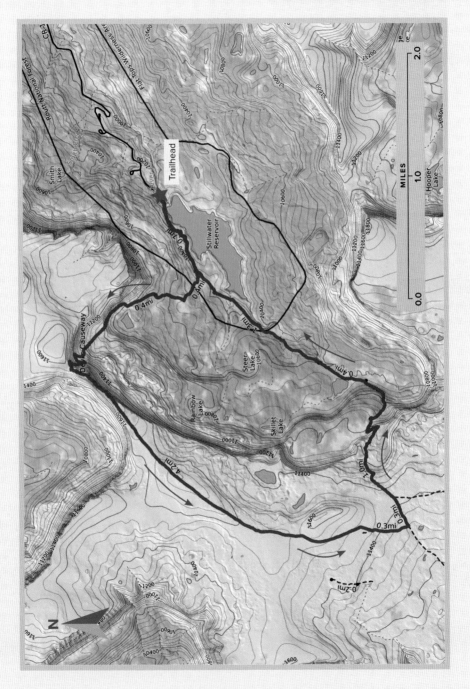

FISH CREEK FALLS

21

Rating	Difficult
Round-Trip Distance	4.8 miles
Elevation Gain	1,400 feet
Round-Trip Time	4 hours
Maps	Trails Illustrated 116: Hahns Peak, Steamboat Lake
Main Attraction	Dense aspen forest and a waterfall

COMMENT: A steady climb through oak, aspen, and fir trees leading to a beautiful waterfall. Start early as this trail can get crowded and hot.

The climb to the falls is rocky and hot.

GETTING THERE: From the town of Steamboat Springs, drive east out of town on Fish Creek Falls Road for 2.4 miles. Fish Creek Falls Road is the road that passes just to the north of the Old Town Hot Springs. Turn right to stay on Fish Creek Falls Road and continue another 0.8 mile to the trailhead.

TRAILHEAD: The Fish Creek Falls Trailhead is a Forest Service fee area. Follow signs for information on how to pay for parking and access to the falls area. At the time I hiked it (2021), the fee was $5. Check the Forest Service website for up-to-date fee information and for any fee-free days.

THE ROUTE: From the upper Fish Creek Falls Trailhead, hike to the Lower Falls Trail. An overlook for the lower falls is accessed by the upper trail leaving from the parking area.

Scrub oak lines the rocky trail.

Descend the trail to the bridge at 0.25 mile and enjoy views of the lower falls before continuing up to the right as the trail climbs steeply on rocks, switchbacking away from the falls. The trail climbs through colorful undergrowth and a mature mixed forest. After a little over a mile, climb steadily through aspens with colorful cliffs above.

At 1.5 miles, enter a pine forest with the sound of the river before crossing a bridge over the water. The trail climbs a couple short but steep rocky sections before finally arriving at Fish Creek Falls at 2.25 miles. It is possible to continue on and view the falls from above (though, obviously, be careful and stay far away from the edge of the falls). You can also scramble down to catch a view of all three levels of the falls. The upper falls are smaller than the more majestic lower falls, but still serve as a rewarding destination for hikers. The upper waterfall has plenty of opportunities for careful exploration and a great spot for a trail lunch before the journey back. The hike back downhill returns the way you came and features some nice views of town.

Upper Fish Creek Falls.

The trail is often rugged and rocky, and you are sure to share the path with a good crowd of hikers. There are sections of ascending 18-inch rocks and obstacles abound in the middle of the trail throughout. I rated the trail "difficult" because of the often-uneven footing and the length. Wear properly fitted and broken-in, supportive footwear for the rocky terrain. The upper parts of the trail are sunny and exposed, so bring adequate sun protection. This hike can also be very hot on a warm day. Steamboat Springs is at a relatively low elevation (6,732 feet) and has an average high temperature of 72°F in September. Take plenty of water and know the limitations of your group. Starting your hike early in the day can help beat the heat and skirt some of the crowds on this extremely popular and iconic fall hike in a majestic part of the state.

Lower Fish Creek Falls is easily accessible and beautiful. The lower waterfall, at 280+ feet, is the second tallest waterfall in the state after Telluride's Bridal Veil Falls. Water flow is at its most tumultuous in the spring-runoff season but still provides a beautiful show in the fall. In the winter and for the properly skilled and equipped, the area is an ice-climbing destination, dependent on conditions.

FISH CREEK FALLS

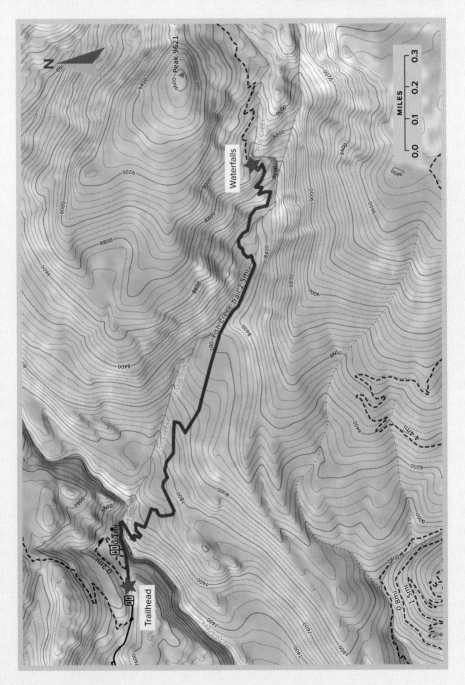

N

Peak 9621

Waterfalls

Fish Creek

Fish Creek Trail 2.5mi

Fish Creek

Fish Creek

0.9mi

0.3mi

Trailhead

4.4mi

0.8mi

1.5mi

Fish Creek

MILES
0.0 0.1 0.2 0.3

FLASH OF GOLD

22

Rating	Difficult
Round-Trip Distance	7.5 miles
Elevation Gain	1,000 feet
Round-Trip Time	6 hours
Maps	Trails Illustrated 117: Clark, Buffalo Pass
Main Attraction	Dense aspen groves with a propensity to turn the full spectrum of colors

COMMENT: A challenging out-and-back up and down the slopes of Buffalo Pass, the hike features old-growth aspens turning a variety of colors. This can be done as a loop or a point-to-point if you station a second car.

GETTING THERE: From Steamboat Springs, take Sixth Street north for 0.7 mile to North Park Road. Follow Strawberry Park Road for a mile and turn left on Park

The upper reaches of the Flash of Gold Trail.

Early morning flashes of gold.

Road. Follow Park Road for 400 feet, turn right onto Strawberry Park Road again, and follow it for 0.8 mile. Turn left at the T junction and follow CR 36 for 4 miles. Turn right onto CR 38 and climb the road for 3.3 miles to the large parking area across from the Dry Lake Campground.

TRAILHEAD: The Buffalo Pass Car Park has plenty of room for recreation users, but on a nice fall day, the lot can fill with mountain bikers and hikers. There are restrooms at the trailhead.

THE ROUTE: From the parking area, start behind the outhouse. The Panorama Trail is an easy loop that departs from here. To avoid going on that loop, stay left at the first two trail junctions and descend to a gated junction at 0.3 mile. Go left at the junction to start climbing the Flash of Gold Trail. At about 0.5 mile, cross a bridge over the creek and continue climbing through a thick and tall aspen grove.

From here, the trail climbs a series of steep switchbacks, passing in and out of a dark mixed conifer and aspen forest. At the 1.5-mile mark, the views open briefly to give a glimpse of the fiery hillsides below, replete with aspens. The views here are a perfect mix between tall colorful canopy and reaching panoramas. Continue

Much of the trail meanders through stretches of colorful undergrowth and tall aspens.

up more switchbacks and enter a section of the hike that isn't quite as steep, briefly dipping into fir forests but mainly wandering under a tall, dense aspen canopy with golden ferns thickly filling the undergrowth. There are some very old trees here as you skirt the edge of a hillside with views beyond the trees.

When you start to get to another series of small switchbacks and can hear the road (after about 3.5–3.7 miles), turn back and descend the way you came. You can also continue to climb most of the way toward Buffalo Pass if you prefer.

A couple of notes: Watch for bikes on this trail. There are plenty of hikers here, but this trail made a name for itself as a mountain biking destination. Also, it is possible to do this hike as a point-to-point if you have a car to station. If you station a car near the turn-around point of the described hike (roughly N40° 31.394' / W106° 45.969'), you can drive back to the parking area. Or vice versa, start at the top and enjoy the descent back to your second vehicle at the Buffalo Pass Car Park. The point-to-point option requires some advanced planning and map-reading skills, but it can be a viable option.

The trail is smooth, packed single-track that has been well maintained for cyclists and hikers alike. Very few rocky sections make this an enjoyable hike with a distinct high ceiling of aspen canopy with colorful undergrowth aplenty. The upper portions of the hike, in particular, are graced with plentiful ferns that turn bright yellow in the fall.

Start early in the day on this south-facing hike and make sure to bring sunscreen for the more exposed sections. Bring plenty of water, especially if you are opting to do this hike as a round trip rather than a shuttle.

This trail is rated as "difficult" due to the length and elevation gain when doing this as a round-trip hike. If you decide to station a car and hike downhill, the hike would be rated as "moderate."

FLASH OF GOLD

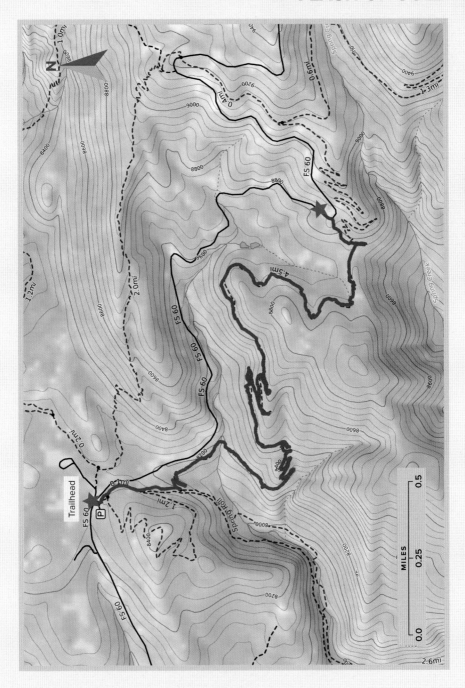

CENTRAL MOUNTAINS

Marcellina Mountain towering above the Kebler grove; Dark Canyon—Kebler Pass (Hike 30).

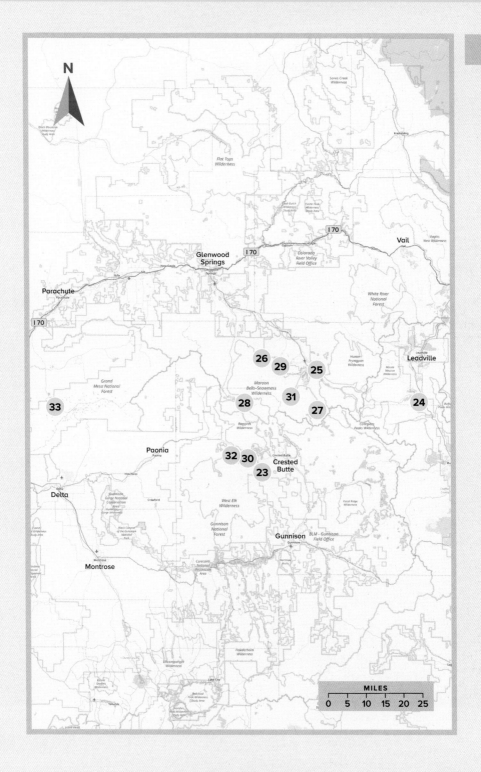

N

Sarvis Creek Wilderness

Black Mountain Wilderness Study Area

Flat Tops Wilderness

Kremmling

I 70

Vail

Eagles Nest Wilderness

Castle Peak Wilderness Study Area

Bull Gulch Wilderness Study Area

Gypsum

Eagle

Colorado River Valley Field Office

Glenwood Springs

I 70

Carbondale

New Castle

Parachute

Parachute

I 70

White River National Forest

Hunter-Fryingpan Wilderness

Mount Massive Wilderness

Leadville

Leadville

Grand Mesa National Forest

26   29   25

Maroon Bells-Snowmass Wilderness

Mt Casco

24

28   31

27

Collegiate Peaks Wilderness

33

Ragged Wilderness

Paonia

Paonia

32 30   Crested Butte

23

Crested Butte

Hotchkiss

Delta

Delta

Gunnison Gorge National Conservation Area

Crawford

West Elk Wilderness

Fossil Ridge Wilderness

Gunnison Gorge Wilderness

Black Canyon of the Gunnison National Park

Gunnison National Forest

Curecanti National Recreation Area

Montrose

Montrose

Gunnison

BLM - Gunnison Field Office

Gunnison

Powderhorn Wilderness

Uncompahgre Wilderness

Lake City

MILES

0   5   10 15 20 25

OHIO PASS BEAVER PONDS

23

Rating	Easy
Round-Trip Distance	1.5 miles
Elevation Gain	300 feet
Round-Trip Time	1 hour
Maps	Trails Illustrated 133: Kebler Pass, Paonia Reservoir
Main Attraction	Aspens galore along an easy hike to a scenic beaver pond lake

COMMENT: A less traveled, easily accessible hike in the crowded Kebler Pass area with endless aspens and scenic picnic spots. A locals' favorite.

GETTING THERE: From Crested Butte, travel west out of town on County Road 12 (Kebler Pass Road) for 6.7 miles. Turn south onto County Road 730 toward Ohio Pass and follow the winding but well-maintained road for 4.2 miles.

TRAILHEAD: The Beaver Ponds Trailhead is on your right and is well signed.

Left: Enter the West Elk Wilderness, a vastly underappreciated expanse. **Right:** Dense aspens with a healthy ecosystem below.

The colors above the beaver ponds are a sight to behold.

THE ROUTE: The trail climbs gently and immediately brings you into the West Elk Wilderness. A series of mild switchbacks takes hikers through dense aspen forests occasionally browsed by cattle. The aspen canopy is dense and dark in these thick woods, and the hike is sometimes muddy. At 0.33 mile, the trail opens up a bit before reentering another dark old-growth aspen forest. Climb to the 0.6-mile mark, where you will emerge to a large beaver pond. The pond has a large lodge forming an island in the middle of the pond, while colorful cliffs of aspen and rock tower above. There is a fun and easy social trail around the edge of the pond that will bring your hiking total to just under a mile before rejoining with the trail you came up. The trail around the pond can also be muddy and a bit of a wet slog, but occasional picnic spots and a change in the view are your reward. The peak above the lake is the Anthracite Range's Ohio Peak.

I rated this hike "easy" because of its short distance and modest elevation gain. A great hike for families with kids, the quiet atmosphere, easy trail on sure footing, and chance of seeing wildlife make this a worthy endeavor that the kids will love. It is also a solid option for those looking for an easy hike that has thinner crowds in the famous Kebler Pass area.

Beavers are common in Colorado, though their presence is mostly detected through observing their ponds and lodges. Their dams are formed by felling trees

Photographers will love this easy hike in the Kebler Pass area.

across creek beds. These primarily aquatic creatures create their dams for shelter and to expand their feeding grounds by creating more standing water. Their work aids plants by growing the riparian areas and by thinning trees. Beaver ponds also help fill aquifers and aid in stabilizing the land. While beaver ponds can sometimes be a nuisance on private land, they are an integral part of Forest Service lands across the state, from the mountains to meadows. Their dams also help filter water, a helpful trait where abandoned mines are present. If you do see a beaver, give it a wide berth. Their sharp teeth cause injury to pets (and occasionally humans) each year. Keep dogs on a leash in areas with beavers, regardless of local regulations for dogs.

OHIO PASS BEAVER PONDS

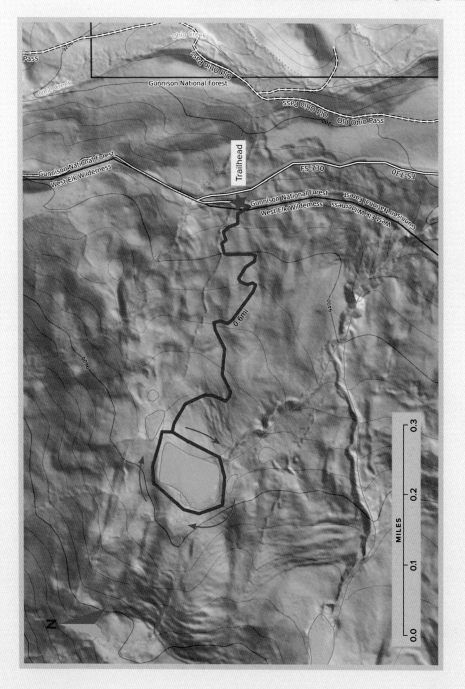

INTERLAKEN— TWIN LAKES

24

Rating	Easy
Round-Trip Distance	4.6 miles
Elevation Gain	150 feet
Round-Trip Time	2.5 hours
Maps	Trails Illustrated 110: Leadville, Fairplay
Main Attraction	Historic buildings amid a colorful, easy hike along the shores of Twin Lakes

COMMENT: Majestic views of Mount Elbert, vibrant slopes, and a history lesson! Diverse plant life includes fragrant sage brush, kinnikinnick, alpine primrose, aspens, and a mixed conifer forest.

GETTING THERE: From Leadville, drive south on US 24 for 14 miles to the junction with CO 82 at the east end of the Twin Lakes. Turn right (west) on CO 82 and drive 0.8 mile to the dirt CR 25, south of the highway. From here, the road is a bit of

The eastern slopes of Mount Elbert towering above the lake into the clouds.

Fragrant sagebrush and aspen.

a choose-your-own-adventure as you navigate campsites and dirt roads all leading to a parking area above the lake. You want to turn west before the Colorado Trail parking area. I had the trailhead marked at N39° 04.45' / W106° 18.62'.

TRAILHEAD: The parking area for the Interlaken Trailhead is an ample space positioned at the end of the dirt road on the Trails Illustrated map. You could also proceed west from the Interlaken Trailhead without much of a change in the route description.

THE ROUTE: From the trailhead, head west on a level, dirt trail above the lake. The path climbs slowly in golden aspen trees for 0.25 mile before joining with the Continental Divide Trail and continuing to hug the lakeshore westward. Undulate gently up and down above the lakeshore (with plenty of picnic spots early on in your hike).

The peak rising above the lake to the north is Mount Elbert (the highest peak in Colorado and the Rockies as a whole), enthroned in aspens, and worthy of a

Mount Elbert and the Twin Lakes.

hike in and of itself. After 1.25 miles, the Colorado Trail branches south off your route and leaves you to continue straight toward incredible views of Mounts Massive and Elbert.

Descend into dense aspens and cross a creek at the 1.95-mile mark. Stay right at the Interlaken sign and approach the historic cabins and remains of Interlaken Resort at the 2.25-mile mark.

Orange aspens on a rainy day.

The historic Interlaken Resort opened in 1879 and closed in the 1950s when the lake was being enlarged, making the resort more isolated. The resort was made into a National Historic District in 1974, and some of the buildings were moved to higher ground as the lake level rose. The remaining buildings are well preserved, and educational signs provide history on the preserved structures, some of which are open to the public to explore inside. The Dexter Cabin, in particular, is open to the public to respectfully explore. James V. Dexter was a wealthy business owner and banker in Colo-

Historic structures in Interlaken.

rado. Dexter built the house in 1895 for his family's use, which was modeled after East Coast high-end homes and features fine hardwoods brought in from the eastern seaboard. The Interlaken Resort fell into disrepair in the years proceeding and immediately after Dexter's death in 1899. A business partner of Dexter's descendants purchased the property in the 1930s and maintained the Dexter Cabin. The remaining resort served as a boarding house until World War I and then sat abandoned and vandalized until being resurrected by the Forest Service to be enjoyed by hikers.

Today, hikers and mountain bikers get to access the historic district via this trail. Enjoy the views, the lake, and the history in this unique crossing of all three. When you are done exploring the town and taking in the views, return the way you came.

INTERLAKEN—TWIN LAKES

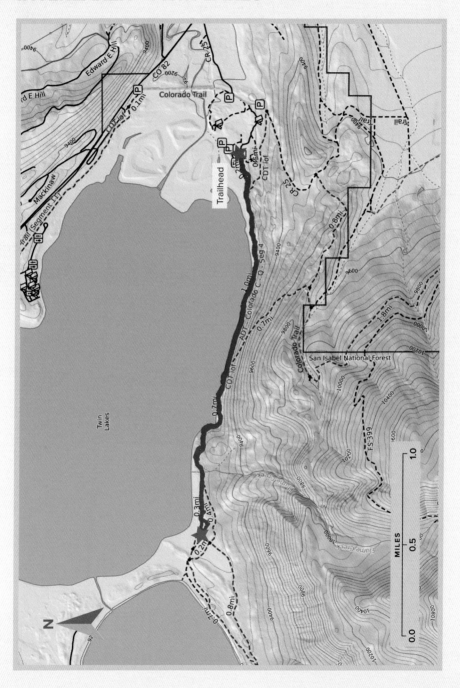

BEHIND THE SIGN TRAIL— SMUGGLER MOUNTAIN OPEN SPACE

25

Rating	Moderate
Round-Trip Distance	3.5 miles
Elevation Gain	1,250 feet
Round-Trip Time	3 hours
Maps	Trails Illustrated 127: Aspen, Independence Pass
Main Attraction	Scrub oak and mine remnants

COMMENT: Panoramic views over the town of Aspen, an old mine archaeological site, and a hike through colorful scrub oak and aspen trees make this one of the more diverse hikes in this book. Combine that with easy driving access and a meal afterward in Aspen and you've got yourself a great option for an afternoon.

The hike climbs a road through scrub oak and aspens.

Big views over the town of Aspen.

GETTING THERE: From Main Street in the town of Aspen, head east to Neal Avenue. Turn right on King Street, then left on Park Circle. In 0.2 mile, take a slight right onto Smuggler Mountain Road.

TRAILHEAD: The Smuggler Mountain Trailhead is at the base of Smuggler Mountain Road. Don't bother trying to drive up the mountain to get closer to the Behind the Sign Trail complex. There is no parking at the top. This is a hiker's road.

THE ROUTE: Hike up the winding dirt road from the parking area to the Smuggler Mountain Trail complex at the top of the hill. The road climbs 750 feet through vibrant Gambel oak turning shades of red and yellow. There are views over the town of Aspen and beyond. Hike this trail early in the day to avoid some of the afternoon heat at this lower elevation. Hiking earlier in the day will also keep the steepest parts of the route in the shade. If you are hiking later in the day, bring plenty of sunscreen for the ascent of Smuggler Mountain.

Gambel oaks are a very important part of the mountain ecosystems in the central part of the state. Wildlife depend on the acorns for food and the dense plant growth for shelter and cover. However, as illustrated by excellent educational signage along the trail, the Gambel oaks here have become overgrown due to a century of fire suppression. Fire is an important part of maintaining a healthy oak ecosystem, and the plants are well adapted to grow back quickly after a blaze. However, currently the oaks are overgrown, creating poor habitat and a fire risk for the nearby town. As such, the city and county are engaged in an effort to cut oaks and open up some of the scrub forest land, creating a healthier ecosystem and thinning fuels so close to town.

Switchback up on the road for 1.4 miles until you reach the Smuggler Mountain Open Space at the top of the road. There is an observation deck at the top with views out over town. Look for the green sign designating the Behind the Sign (BTS) Trail. Proceed, behind the sign, climbing the trail through short, dense aspens, switching to lodgepole pines 0.25 mile in to the BTS trail. Long pants are recommended on this trail due to the dense growth habits of trees all throughout this hike. At the 1.9-mile mark (from the parking lot), take the signed cutoff to Bushwacker Mine.

The mine site has the modest remains of a historic mining operation along with benches and flat open space for rest and exploration. The mine once occupied

The trail takes on a wild feel after leaving the overlooks and the road.

Approaching the mine ruins.

20 acres and had many of the treatments of a full-fledged town. The Bushwacker extracted silver until the silver crash of 1893 halted operations. The mine resumed extracting ore in 1898 and continued into the early 1900s until decaying infrastructure made the venture unprofitable. Today, the site serves as an interesting stop on this unique hike leaving from the middle of the bustling streets of Aspen.

To get back to the Smuggler Mountain Open Space complex, descend the wide trail, down the double-track trail from the mine for 0.3 mile to the Smuggler Mountain Road. Turn right to descend the road and return to the car the way you came up.

This trail is rated as "moderate" because of its steep grade on a well-maintained trail. At the top of the hiking road, the trail network can get a bit overgrown and less marked. This is a large network of trails on generally stable footing but some routefinding skills may be necessary to navigate the numerous social trails in this popular area. Also of note, if you plan on camping in the surrounding area before or after your hike, Aspen is a notoriously difficult place to find a last-minute camping spot. It is highly recommended that you plan ahead and reserve a space in one of the local campgrounds. If you are aiming for dispersed camping, one of the few limited options may be found off Independence Pass Road in the Lincoln Creek area.

BEHIND THE SIGN TRAIL—
SMUGGLER MOUNTAIN OPEN SPACE

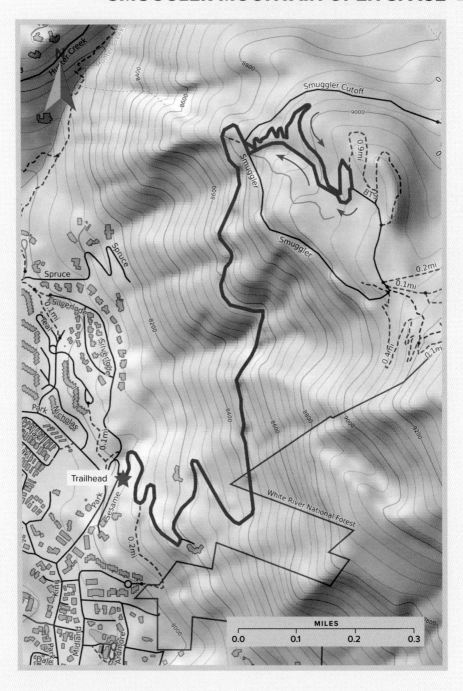

CAPITOL CREEK

26

Rating	Difficult
Round-Trip Distance	5.25 miles
Elevation Gain	1,200 feet
Round-Trip Time	4 hours
Maps	Trails Illustrated 128: Maroon Bells, Redstone, Marble
Main Attraction	Quintessential aspen views under one of Colorado's most majestic 14ers

COMMENT: Hit this hike at peak color and it is hard to beat statewide for the most vibrantly colorful hikes around.

GETTING THERE: From Aspen, drive 13 miles northwest on CO 82 to the town of Snowmass. Turn left onto Capitol Creek Road. After 1.7 miles, turn right to stay on Capitol Creek Road and continue just shy of 8 miles to the trailhead. The final mile of the road is a narrow four-wheel-drive road that requires high clearance.

Though this hike is about big views, the enclosed, forested sections are also gorgeous.

TRAILHEAD: The Capitol Creek Trailhead is a busy spot with hunters, hikers, and anglers.

THE ROUTE: Hiking this trail counterclockwise will provide the best views of the Capitol Creek drainage and all its aspen glory. From the trailhead, follow the ditch trail southwest with immediate views of Capitol Peak and the aspen wonderland of the Capitol Creek Trail spread out before you.

At the 0.5-mile mark, enter a large old-growth aspen grove. The trail is flat and beautiful before starting to climb at the

A sea of aspens spread out beneath Capitol Peak.

1-mile mark. Cross a small creek and enter the Maroon Bells Snowmass Wilderness at the 1.45-mile mark. Cross an open meadow and begin to undulate up and down in aspens again.

The views open up, and this is close to Colorado fall hiking at its finest. The jagged edges of Capitol Peak and Mount Daly rise above expansive colorful forests. At 2.8 miles, you'll reach a beautiful creek delta and the southernmost point on your hike. From here, cross the creek and begin your return to the parking lot by descending sharply through a mixed forest, young aspens, and creek crossings. Cross a bridge and start climbing back to the parking lot through scrub oak. Once at the road, navigate left back to your car.

The majestic peaks over the hike are some of Colorado's tallest. Mount Daly, at 13,300 feet, is an integral part of the scenery of Snowmass ski area, Aspen, and beyond. Capitol Peak, at 14,137 feet, is in the Maroon Bells–Snowmass Wilderness and rises 7,500 feet above the Roaring Fork Valley. The peak is known as one of

The ridges above the Capitol Creek meadows on a misty fall morning.

Colorado's hardest 14er ascents. The northeast ridge of Capitol Peak features the infamously difficult "Knife's Edge"—a narrow ridge that asks climbers to brave dramatic exposure and loose rock to reach the summit. Annually, this is among the deadliest 14er routes. From the relative safety of the Capitol Creek Trail, however, the ultra-prominent peak makes for one of the most beautiful hikes in this collection.

Other noteworthy points of interest on this hike are the occasional arborglyph and various tree species, primarily aspens, oaks, and willows, that create a vibrant diversity of colors and extend the fall colors season due to their slightly different color schedules. The hike has a number of sections of open areas that require sun protection, such as sunglasses, sunscreen, and UPF clothing.

I rated this hike as a "difficult" because it climbs over 1,000 feet and crosses the 5-mile mark in length. If you do not want to do the full loop, the rating could be lowered. It is also important to stay on route. Some online maps show a cut-off spur trail that skips the creek crossing at the hike's apex. I did not see that spur in the field, but there are a number of social trails in the area. Because of the multitude of smaller trails on the hike, routefinding is an important skill to have in your hiking toolkit here, and an added layer of difficulty to the hike.

CAPITOL CREEK

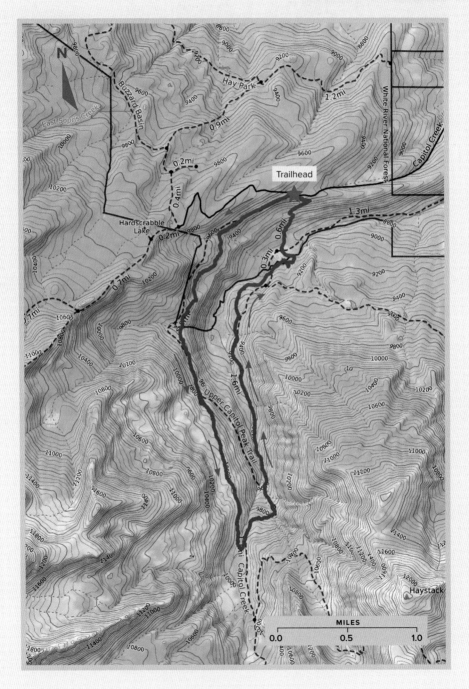

CATHEDRAL LAKE

27

Rating	Difficult
Round-Trip Distance	5.6 miles
Elevation Gain	1,993 feet
Round-Trip Time	4.5 hours
Maps	Trails Illustrated 127: Aspen, Independence Pass
Main Attraction	Dense aspens and a majestic alpine lake

COMMENT: A challenging climb to an alpine cirque, this hike flashes fall colors above and below tree line.

GETTING THERE: From Aspen, drive west to the traffic circle with the Castle Creek Road. Drive south on Castle Creek Road for 12 miles. Turn right on Castle Creek Road. The dirt road up to the trailhead is 0.6 mile long and is a high-clearance road.

The approach to this lake has plenty of color. Photo by Jeff Golden

TRAILHEAD: The Cathedral Lake Trailhead is a fifteen-car trailhead parking area after a short rough road. Small SUVs should be fine to navigate the 0.6-mile road to the trailhead.

THE ROUTE: From the Cathedral Lake Trailhead, hike up through dense aspen trees that create a thick canopy of color. The trees occasionally part enough to afford a view of a lit-up hillside and the lake amphitheater that is your hike destination.

At 0.5 mile, the trail turns away from the valley you drove in on and up the drainage that empties the lakes above. The trail climbs through a pine forest through rocky footing, with the sounds of a creek and cascades below.

The trail climbs steadily for the entire length of the hike, traversing the dense aspen grove

Looking down on the first sections of the trail. Photo by Jeff Golden

throughout the lower reaches. At 0.75 mile, enter the Maroon Bells–Snowmass Wilderness. Proceed upward onto a scree field just shy of a mile.

When I did this hike in 2022, the area was in the midst of an aspen leaf miner outbreak, which can affect fall color. But that's no reason to skip the hike, even if the blight continues.

The trail continues to climb through young aspens so dense that hiking partners are out of view just a hundred feet away at times. Catch glimpses of the majesty uphill and keep climbing through quick switchbacks. At 1.25 miles, there is a rushing cascade with a social trail down to inspect the waters. Keep climbing the switchbacks toward your goal.

The climb gives views of the willows and creek below with an aspen-laden hillside and tundra grasses alight in color above. At 2.25 miles, the trail begins to climb some of the steepest switchbacks around. Take your time and stay left at the top of the switchbacks. Be very careful not to kick any rocks down on hikers below. Take a page out of climbers' books and yell "rock" (or similar) if you accidentally send something careening down.

Descend briefly and then climb through dispersed camping spots among the willows. At 2.5 miles, the trail crosses the creek on any number of social trails. Choose the trail that continues climbing until reaching the lake at 2.8 miles. Enjoy the numerous social trails around the lake, rest up from your steep climb, eat lunch, or have a snack. Then descend the way you came.

Cathedral Lake

The lake amphitheater is visible, and beautiful, for the last mile or so. Photo by Jeff Golden

Cathedral Lake sits at 11,864 feet and features beautiful turquoise-colored waters. Cathedral Peak, at 13,950 feet, towers over the lake to the northeast. The easiest way to explore higher in the valley is by backtracking and taking the Electric Pass Trail, which will get you to the ridge above the lakes.

I rated this hike "difficult" because of its steady climb and above-moderate mileage. The switchback section just below the lake, in particular, is steep, loose, and aggressive. The high elevation makes the air thin, and the aerobic exercise is real. Take your time and enjoy the valley views, both above and below.

A canopy of aspens. Photo by Jeff Golden

There are plentiful options for fall hikes in the (aptly named) Aspen area. This is a fantastic option for anyone looking for more of a workout over the shorter or more moderate hikes in Aspen proper, near the Maroon Bells Lakes, or on the Snowmass resort.

CATHEDRAL LAKE

CRYSTAL MILL

28

Rating	Moderate
Round-Trip Distance	9.5 miles
Elevation Gain	1,300 feet
Round-Trip Time	9 hours
Maps	Trails Illustrated 128: Maroon Bells, Redstone, Marble
Main Attraction	Unbeatable fall color and clear water at a historic site

COMMENT: This iconic hike ends at the incredibly photogenic Crystal Mill, an old powerhouse for nearby mines.

GETTING THERE: From Carbondale, drive south on CO 133 for 20 miles. The turnoff for the small town of Marble is just south of the Gunnison County line. Turn left and drive east on CO 133 south past the Bogan Flats Campground and toward

Hiking the jeep road to the mill.

Marble. Continue for 8 miles into the town of Marble. Follow Main Street through town toward the reservoir east of town. Continue on the road north of the lake to a small road-side parking area before the road turns into an unmaintained four-wheel-drive route. Note that this hike can technically be driven all the way to the mill. So, you may drive until you feel like the progressively worsening road conditions impede, but this hike write-up begins from the parking area at the edge of town. Do not block private residences and follow all parking regulations.

TRAILHEAD: The town of Marble sits at the launching-off point for the four-wheel-drive road to the mill. Park out of the way of nearby driveways at the pullout at approximately N 39° 04.29' / W107° 10.27'.

The creek and valley approach would be enough to include this hike in the book, even apart from the mill.

THE ROUTE: From the parking area at the edge of town, hike up the rough road to a junction with a sign pointing to the town of Crystal. From here on out, you're better off hiking. For one, the route is beautiful. For another, this is a rough road with four-wheel-drive and some nerves required. Go down a small hill and cross a creek at 1 mile. Pass the placid Lizard Lake at 1.2 miles and proceed on with cliffs and fall color draping the hillsides above. The trail follows the Crystal River with flaming hillsides of aspens alight above. At the 1.75-mile mark, cross some wet spots in the trail and climb away from the river. Rejoin the creek at the 2.9-mile mark. This area of the trail passes through private property and a diverse forest full of evergreen pine and cottonwood color. Spot a waterfall high on the hillside a mile from the mill and continue on to one of the most scenic spots in the state, the famed Crystal Mill. There is a small fee to descend to the creek bed for the most scenic and iconic photos of the mill, but the vistas are astounding no matter where you end up. Take your time enjoying the area and learning about the history of the town and mill site, and return the way you came.

Crystal Mill

The Crystal Mill in all its fall majesty.

The Crystal Mill was built in 1893 along the Crystal River as a power station with a waterwheel that powered an air compressor. Compressed-air-powered drills were used for placing dynamite in the nearby Sheep Mountain and Bear Mountain silver mines. The mill closed in 1917, landed on the National Register of Historic Places in 1985, and today has become one of the most photographed places in Colorado, particularly in the autumn.

The town of Marble is one of the more unique mountain towns in the state. Yards and ditches are littered with blocks of marble from the nearby mine. The high-quality stone from the region has been used to build a number of famous monuments thousands of miles away in Washington, DC, including the Tomb of the Unknown Soldier and the Lincoln Memorial.

I rated this hike "moderate" because of its longer length that still stays under 10 miles. The road is rocky and an extremely difficult drive. Most people hike it, and you will be happier, and less sore afterward, if you do that. Seeing as feet are easier to maneuver around large boulders, on foot, the trail surface is not overly punishing to navigate. While you can get by without making this hike overly difficult, this is no easy hike. So be patient and assess your fitness level before embarking.

Hikers can pay a fee to access the creek bed for pictures like this.

CRYSTAL MILL

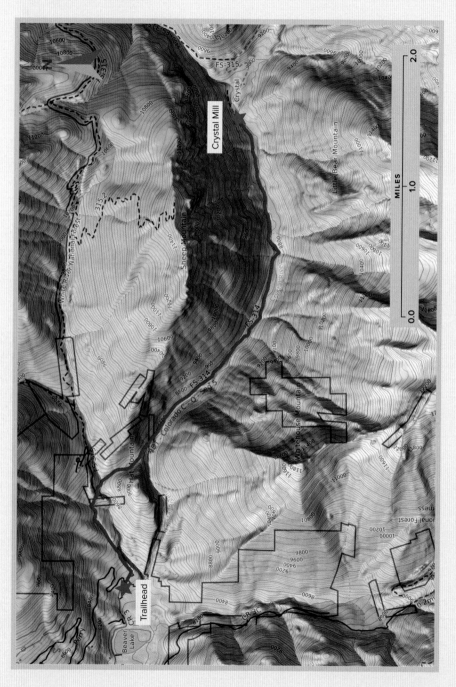

DITCH TRAIL—
SNOWMASS

29

Rating	Easy
Round-Trip Distance	1.6 miles
Elevation Gain	350 feet
Round-Trip Time	1 hour
Maps	Trails Illustrated 128: Maroon Bells, Redstone, Marble
Main Attraction	Easy hiking with views of aspens and Mount Daly

COMMENT: This easy trek combines easy access (paved roads within the resort complex), flat and clean trails, leaf peeping, and views of 13,300-foot Mount Daily to the west.

GETTING THERE: From the town of Snowmass, travel south on CO 82 for 8.4 miles. Turn right (west) onto Brush Creek Road, continuing through roundabouts and through Snowmass Village. At 5.2 miles, turn right onto County Road 10. After 1 mile, turn left onto Divide Road and then immediately take a right onto Piñon Drive to the parking area on your right.

TRAILHEAD: The Ditch Trailhead is a ski resort parking area with plenty of space. There are no restroom facilities. If you do not want to drive, there is a free shuttle that carries hikers and cyclists to the various trails across the resort area. For more information, contact Snowmass Village Transportation at 970-923-3500.

THE ROUTE: This flat and well-maintained trail heads west from the parking area across the west edge of the ski resort along an old irrigation ditch. Pass through old-growth

In just a few weeks, the trail you're hiking will see skiers flying downhill.

Mount Daly towers above the Ditch Trail.

aspens to a wide-open view around 0.25 mile. At 0.5 mile, hike under the Campground Lift with views of a colorful hillside to the right (north).

At 0.75 mile, enter a pine forest before emerging to expansive views north and west. At 0.9 mile, a bench is positioned in a prime place to view 12,300-foot Mount Daly and the Snowmass Creek Valley.

Mount Daly owes a lot of its beauty to its almost 800 feet of prominence. Prominence is a measure of how high a mountain "sticks out" above surrounding peaks, measured as the height of a peak relative to the lowest contour line fully encircling that peak. Prominent peaks are the ones that tend to draw your eye and make you want to lace up your boots!

If you look closely at Mount Daly, you can see a wide diagonal "stripe" across the mountain. This is what geologists call an igneous intrusion. It is a different kind of rock, volcanic in origin, that forced its way into a gash in the middle of the older rock making up the rest of the mountain. While geology is certainly not my area of expertise, the visual appeal of Mount Daly is certainly augmented by interesting details such as the characteristic stripe.

Turn around to return the way you came. If you want to keep hiking, leave the fall foliage and climb south past the bench. There are opportunities to do a loop by combining your hike with a trip up the hill via the Government Trail to the Campground Trail, switchbacking down the hill to the Ditch Trail again.

This hike is under the jurisdiction of the town of Snowmass. As such, it is required that dogs be on leash at all times.

I rated this hike "easy" because of its level footing, mild elevation gains, and low mileage. As with most easy hikes in this book, there are ways to make the hike more challenging. If you choose to climb and continue on, making the hike into a loop, carry a map and be prepared for a "moderate" hike. Otherwise, this is a spectacular hike for families with young children or for those visiting from a low elevation and looking for a mild, scenic afternoon.

The valley below Mount Daly is a sight to behold.

DITCH TRAIL—SNOWMASS

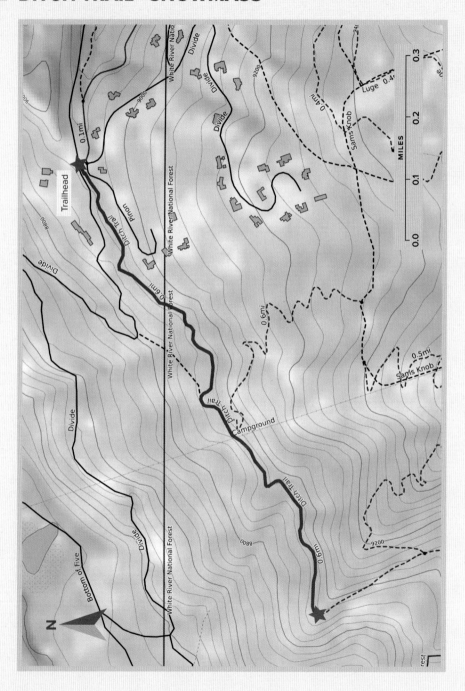

DARK CANYON—KEBLER PASS

30

Rating	Moderate
Round-Trip Distance	4.1 miles
Elevation Gain	800 feet
Round-Trip Time	3 hours
Maps	Trails Illustrated 133: Kebler Pass, Paonia Reservoir
Main Attraction	One of the most majestic areas of Colorado every fall, this hike leads to a high overlook

COMMENT: Perhaps my favorite fall hike in this entire book, this trek combines history, ecology, and incredible vistas that make it worth braving the crowds.

GETTING THERE: From the town of Crested Butte, drive west on White Rock Avenue as it heads out of town and becomes County Road 12 (Kebler Pass Road). Take the road for 12 miles and look for signs for Horse Ranch Park. There are lots of scenic pullouts and turnoffs with exploring, so you may want to build in some extra time for the drive.

TRAILHEAD: The Horse Ranch Park Trailhead is situated on the edge of a large open meadow full of the hustle and bustle of leaf peepers. Expect a crowded party atmosphere with people grilling and gearing up for adventures in all directions from this centrally located trailhead in the heart of the Kebler Pass aspen colony. The trailhead is on the north side of the road by the outhouses, and the trailhead signs are about a 0.1-mile hike up the road past the gate.

Take a load off.

The views from this overlook are among the best I found in the state.

COLORADO'S BEST HIKES FOR FALL COLORS

THE ROUTE: From the outhouses, hike north along the dirt road for 0.25 mile until reaching the Dark Canyon Trail 830 signpost; to the right is the Dyke Creek Trail. For this hike, stay left on the Dark Canyon Trail toward Oh-Be-Joyful Pass. The trail climbs gently before dropping into a grove of aspens and then an open meadow with extraordinary views of the surrounding peaks and unmatched fall colors. Take a moment to enjoy the meadow and the views of the East Beckwith Mountain massif, the prominent mountain to the southwest. Leaving the meadow, begin to climb a bit steeper and pay attention to the old-growth aspens here. Many of them bear the carvings of visitors from the 1950s. At the 1-mile mark, cross a talus field with incredible views out across the Kebler aspen grove. This is a hike filled with views that make you feel small. Enjoy the majesty of the mountains rising above what truly looks like an ocean of trees.

Continue to climb until the 1.3-mile mark where you will cross a series of beaver ponds. Signs of an active beaver population abound, and if you do happen to see any of the creatures, give them a wide berth (especially if you have any dogs with you). To the northeast, 13,058-foot Mount Owen and 12,644-foot Ruby Peak rise above the picturesque beaver meadows. This area can get a bit swampy, but the late season should make bugs a nonissue. Be prepared for a wet slog through the low-lying beaver-pond area before climbing gradually out of the meadows and into the most extraordinary part of the hike. Just past the 1.5-mile mark, keep your head up and look around for arborglyphs and some truly massive aspen trees. The gradually

"Home sweet home."

climbing meadows here house the largest aspen trees I've seen in Colorado. By my amateur measurements, I found some trees over 3 feet in diameter. I spent over an hour in this section of the trail wandering around the open areas punctuated by these champion-sized trees.

Judging by the carvings on the trees, this was clearly the home to many sheepherders from the likes of Peru, El Salvador, and more ranging from the early 1940s to the 1970s. Look closely and you can see the same sets of names carved into trees with dates spanning many seasons. A homesick carving of South America, etched by a Peruvian in the 1980s graces one tree, while elegant-scripted initials and a crudely drawn sheep is visible on another. Perhaps my favorite tree carving in the area came from a simple "JHK" who left their initials with dates from the summers of 1941, 1942, and 1943 next to the simple words "Home Sweet Home." For more information on arborglyphs in Colorado, see the introduction.

When you decide to move on from the hallway of historical trees, climb the final section to a jaw-dropping overlook at the 2-mile mark. Here you will find a collection of granite that forms the top of a cliff with views for upward of 40 miles. The Kebler aspen grove spreads out below, reaching all the way to views of Marcellina Mountain. The Kebler aspen grove is the largest in the state, and some scientists have argued that this grove is the largest living organism on earth! See the introduction for more info on the clonal nature of aspens. Take some pictures and enjoy the best season of the year in one of the best spots in the state, and head back the way you came.

I found this hike to be of moderate intensity due to its 4 miles of spread-out gradual climbs and descents. The trail is well-marked and, aside from the muddy beaver ponds section, easy to hike with clean boots.

DARK CANYON—KEBLER PASS

MAROON BELLS

31

Rating	Moderate
Round-Trip Distance	3.5 miles
Elevation Gain	775 feet
Round-Trip Time	3 hours
Maps	Trails Illustrated 128: Maroon Bells, Redstone, Marble
Main Attraction	The most photographed place in the state can't possibly live up to the hype, right? Incorrect. This place is incredible, especially in the fall.

COMMENT: An incredibly busy trail that requires some planning ahead to visit, this moderate hike is well worth the work to secure the permits and brave the crowds.

GETTING THERE: From Aspen, drive west on Main Street to CO 82. At the first roundabout, take the second exit onto Maroon Creek Road. Continue 1.5 miles to the Aspen Highlands turnout on your left.

The Maroon Bells loom large above Crater Lake.

TRAILHEAD: The Maroon Lake Trailhead is accessed by the Maroon Bells shuttle bus station in the Aspen Highlands ski resort parking area. Parking is paid by the half hour, so brace your wallet for Aspen parking prices. Proceed upstairs to the shuttle bus check-in.

Note that these directions are reflective of conditions as they were when I hiked this in the fall of 2022. Consult the town of Aspen's online resources for up-to-date information on Maroon Bells reservations, parking, and regulations. This hike is almost sure to require a reservation on the shuttle bus. Shuttle bus tickets are an additional fee.

THE ROUTE: The shuttle bus drops riders off at the top of the paved road. There are restrooms and

The Maroon Bells from the lower lake.

a small ranger station with interpretive signs. Proceed to the bench just below the restrooms and begin your hike here at the top of the paved trails.

Descend the trail toward the lower lake and take a moment to take in the iconic view that you've seen a million times before in photos. The Maroon Bells rise above Maroon Lake, enthroned in aspens and colorful grasses. This is a view that I had seen in photos a thousand times. I didn't think it would live up to the hype. This view is better than the pictures you will take. Take the pics anyway and tell your friends to do this hike.

From the Maroon Lake shore, climb the valley on the paved trail to the sign where the hike turns into a dirt trail, climbing the valley away from the paved sections. From the bench behind the restrooms, the trail enters the Maroon Bells Wilderness area after 0.5 mile.

The entire amphitheater is majestic. Photo by Mario Rangel

The trail climbs steadily on a rough, rocky trail through a scree field with gorgeous views of the peaks above. The trail is crowded throughout. However, it is shaded with dense aspen groves for most of the way. The trail is steep and rocky with periodic views of the peaks above.

At 1.75 miles, turn left at the Crater Lake sign and begin to descend to the upper lake. Depending on how much snow and rain has fallen in the season you're hiking, the lake level may be high or low. Regardless, Crater Lake offers a majestic view of the Maroon Bells above. Aspen trees ring the right (north) side of the amphitheater while 14,025-foot Pyramid Peak rises to the south.

The major peaks above the lake are North Maroon Peak to the north and Maroon Peak to the south. The unconsolidated nature of the rock of these peaks makes them some of the most difficult 14ers to climb. The rotten rock has given these peaks the name "the Deadly Bells" for their reputation as dangerous climbing destinations.

I rated this hike "moderate" for its middling distance and elevation gain. This is a well-marked trail, but do not be fooled. This is still a hike. Don't wear your brand-new white sneakers on this jaunt. Be prepared for a trek through mud, ice, and rock.

Return the way you came after enjoying the gorgeous Crater Lake. The shuttle bus system and the crowds may be annoying, but preserving this area from over-crowding is worth the hassle.

MAROON BELLS

THREE LAKES LOOP— KEBLER PASS

32

Rating	Easy
Round-Trip Distance	3.7 miles
Elevation Gain	560 feet
Round-Trip Time	3 hours
Maps	Trails Illustrated 133: Kebler Pass, Paonia Reservoir
Main Attraction	Alpine lakes on an easy hike!

COMMENT: Another classic hike in the Kebler Pass area, this hike is a local favorite but doesn't attract as many crowds as some of the other hikes in the area. This is a fantastic hike with mixed vegetation, colorful understory ferns and grasses alight in fall color, and the variety of forested hiking, bubbling cascades, and placid lakes.

GETTING THERE: From Crested Butte, drive west on County Road 12 (Kebler Pass Road) for 15.9 miles. Turn left (south) onto County Road 706 toward Lost Lake Campground. Take this well-maintained forest road for 2.5 miles and park in the Beckwith Pass Trail parking area. The campground just past the Beckwith Pass Trailhead is a fee area. All day-use vehicles in the campground need to pay. However, the Beckwith parking area is free to use.

Climbing the trail above the first of the three lakes.

Marcellina Mountain north of the lakes.

TRAILHEAD: The Beckwith Pass Trailhead is a small gravel parking area just outside of the paid campground. Park on one of the gravel lots and avoid paying for parking or camping.

THE ROUTE: From the Beckwith Trail (842) parking area, follow the trail leaving the east side of the parking area. The trail begins by climbing gently through a fir forest and across a creek. At 0.4 mile, stay left to avoid going into the campground. Proceed for another 0.1 mile and take the junction to the right (south) to begin hiking on the Three Lakes Trail (843).

Once on the Three Lakes Trail, the path begins to climb steadily through switchbacks and one last rocky push toward the junction with the Dollar Lake spur at the top of the hill. On the climb up to the trail junction, enjoy views of the Lost Lake Slough (the largest of the three lakes and the one closest to the campground). The surrounding hills are ablaze with yellow aspens punctuating dense fir forests. Looking back down the hill you're climbing, the large dome-shaped mountain to the northwest is Marcellina Mountain.

At the top of the hill, a signed junction at 1.25 miles points hikers toward Dollar Lake, a small but scenic lake shaped like a dollar coin. The Dollar Lake detour is 0.25 mile to the lake and then 0.25 mile back to the junction with the regular trail. The crest of the trail just before Dollar Lake is the high-elevation point of the hike. Continue your hike after Dollar Lake by rejoining the main trail and turning west (left) where you will begin to descend toward the second of the three lakes on the tour.

Lost Lake is the middle child of the lakes: bigger than Dollar Lake but not as large as Slough at the bottom of the trio. To get there, continue your descent from the Dollar Lake junction, passing a small cascade at 1.75 miles and finding Lost Lake through the trees at 2 miles. Continue past the lake and descend through a pine forest.

The trail begins to switchback on the descent at 2.5 miles and deposits you in the Lost Lake campground at 2.8 miles. Take a moment to appreciate the peaks towering over Lost Lake Slough to the south. The massif is East Beckwith Mountain.

To get back to your car, hike along the road north out of the campground to the Beckwith Trail parking area.

I rated this hike "easy" because of its modest elevation gains and its shorter mileage. Some may find this to be a moderate hike because it is over 3 miles. But the trail is only briefly steep, and there is an option to shorten the mileage by cutting out the Dollar Lake detour. The footing is rocky and more challenging than most "easy" hikes in this book. This is a good choice for those visiting the Kebler Pass area who want an easier hike than the Dark Canyon out-and-back but that is more challenging than the Ohio Pass Beaver Ponds.

Looking south from the lower lake.

THREE LAKES LOOP—KEBLER PASS

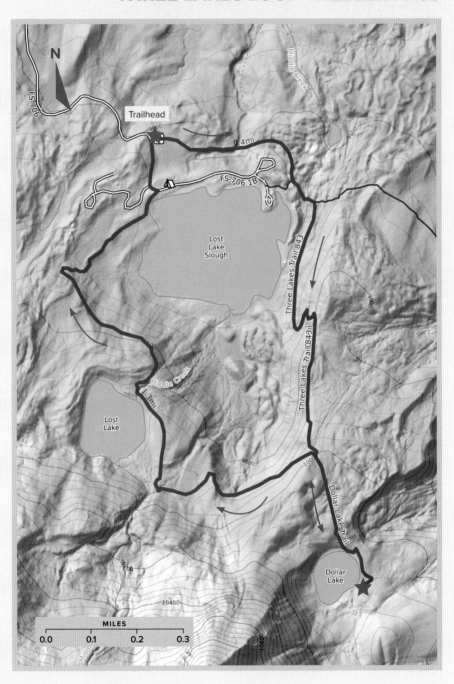

GRAND MESA LAKES

33

Rating	Moderate
Round-Trip Distance	3.3 miles
Elevation Gain	495 feet
Round-Trip Time	3 hours
Maps	Trails Illustrated 136: Grand Mesa
Main Attraction	Unique topography, giant aspens, and a lodge to grab a drink after the hike

COMMENT: The Grand Mesa is one of Colorado's most interesting areas, and this hike is a great sampling of this unique geographic area.

GETTING THERE: From Grand Junction, drive east on Interstate 70 to Exit 49, signed for Colorado 65 south toward Grand Mesa and Collbran.

TRAILHEAD: For the Mesa Lakes Trailhead, take Colorado 65 toward the Grand Mesa for 24.8 miles. Pass Powderhorn ski area and just past the brown sign for the Mesa Lakes Recreation Area, turn right on Forest Service Road 252 and arrive at

A scree field on the far side of the lower lake.

Crossing the boardwalk to circle the lower lake.

the federal fee area with the lodge and the trailhead. The federal fee area charged $6 at the time of publication for day use.

THE ROUTE: From the Mesa Lakes Trailhead, take a moment to survey the area. Finding the right starting point can be a bit difficult as this area is dotted with small lakes and social trails. Start at the trailhead restroom and follow the trail behind the privy toward the largest of the lakes in the area, horseshoe-shaped Mesa Lake. Follow the sign toward Lost Lake. Skirt the west end of Mesa Lake, hiking south.

After 0.25 mile, turn right (west-southwest) to join Lost Lake 502 Trail. The trail climbs gently through fragrant pine with the occasional aspen colony flashing yellow colors and dropping a colorful carpet of leaves on the trail. There are some enormous old aspens on this trail interspersed throughout the pine forest. At 0.5 mile, keep left to continue on the Lost Lake 502 Trail. The trail skirts South Mesa Lake and continues to climb once leaving the lake shore.

The trail switchbacks briefly as you approach 1 mile and the top of the hike. Descend steeply to the shores of Lost Lake. Yes, another "Lost Lake." This edition of the Colorado "Lost Lake" is a narrow puddle nestled between picturesque grey scree fields, stately pines, and a collection of large boulders.

Return the way you climbed up to Lost Lake. After descending back toward Mesa Lake, turn right (east) when you get back to Mesa Lake at 2 miles. The meandering trail around Mesa Lake will deposit you back at your car but not before

The climb to the upper lake features some old-growth aspens.

carrying you through a scree field with gorgeous views of orange and red aspens all around the lake bay. At 3 miles, cross a sturdy wooden bridge and begin to watch for the cutoff back to the privy and trailhead parking lot.

Of the three lakes, the lowest lake, Mesa Lake, has the most vibrant fall colors, followed by South Mesa Lake and then Lost Lake.

I rated this hike "moderate" because of the condition of the footing. While the trail length and elevation gain are not daunting, the trail surface is filled with larger protruding rocks, and there's some loose footing at the top of the trek near Lost Lake. There are opportunities to shave mileage off the total by skipping the Mesa Lake loop or by only doing the easy Mesa Lake loop shoreline trail.

The Grand Mesa is a fascinating place in the western part of the state. "Grand mesa" is Spanish for "large table," and this one is the largest flat-topped mountain in the world. It has an area of 500 square miles and is a mix of federal forest lands and private resorts. The top of the mesa has more than three hundred lakes and is home to large aspen forests. The north side of the mountain slope is covered with dense oak stands, alight with red and orange fall color.

Dots of orange, yellow, and green above one of the Mesa Lakes.

GRAND MESA LAKES

N

Sunset
Lake

0.2mi

0.2mi

Summer Homes

Mesa Lakes
0.2mi

9800

10000

CO 65

Beaver
Lake

10000

0.1mi

Trailhead

Mesa Creek

1.1mi

Mesa
Lake

10000

South
Mesa
Lake

Lost Lake Trail 0.9mi

10000

10200

Lost
Lake

10200

10200

10400

10200

MILES

0.0   0.1   0.2   0.3

SOUTHERN MOUNTAINS

Mount Sneffels towers above low-lying aspens (Hike 40).

JUD WIEBE MEMORIAL TRAIL

34

Rating	Moderate
Round-Trip Distance	3.4 miles
Elevation Gain	1,300 feet
Round-Trip Time	3 hours
Maps	Trails Illustrated 141: Telluride, Silverton, Ouray, Lake City
Main Attraction	Aspens and panoramic views

COMMENT: The Jud Wiebe Memorial Trail is a moderate trail starting and ending in the town of Telluride. Named for a late Forest Service ranger, the trail climbs out of town and offers panoramic views of the golden hillsides above Telluride.

GETTING THERE: The trail begins at the end of North Aspen Street in downtown Telluride. From "main street" (CO 145, Colorado Avenue), turn north on Aspen Street and continue until the road ends, near West Dakota Avenue. Follow parking regulations, as there are no parking areas and metered sites. This is also a residential area, so be wary of blocking anyone's driveway and respect residents' privacy.

Aspens competing for sunlight and attention as leaves turn.

TRAILHEAD: The Jud Wiebe Trailhead is nestled at the end of Aspen Street near some condos. Look for the large trail marker interpretive sign.

THE ROUTE: At the north end of Aspen Street, look for interpretive signage and a bridge signed as "Jud Wiebe Trail No. 432." Cross the bridge over the creek and climb steadily with views of town to your left. Enter a tall, dense aspen grove at the first switchback at 0.6 mile. Hike along the rocky trail under the golden canopy as the forest gets thicker. The trail temporarily levels out slightly just shy of 0.9 mile before meeting the Deep Creek Trail junction.

Keep right to stay on the Jud Wiebe Trail. At 1.2 miles is a bench with panoramic views back into

Climbing above Telluride.

town and around the colorful hillsides. This is a good place to catch your breath before meeting the high point of the trail at 1.36 miles.

Hike on, descending slowly from the panoramic views before entering another thick aspen grove. At this point, take a moment to appreciate the fact that while you may feel like you are deep in the mountains, you are still within city limits.

There is a small creek crossing at 2 miles. Continue steeply downward on loose rock before entering scrub oak (with an accompanying splash of red) and reaching the east trailhead at 3 miles. Turn right (west) to walk down Tomboy Road back toward your car. At this point, back in town, there are numerous ways to get back to the original trailhead or your parking spot. Consult the city block map to get back to your vehicle!

The Jud Wiebe Trail was named after a US Forest Service employee who designed the trail but passed away in 1986 before the trail construction was completed. Wiebe worked in Norwood, Colorado, from 1980 to 1986 and proposed, laid out, and broke ground on the trail before his death. Volunteers finished the trail construction after his death. Wiebe is memorialized with a plaque at the top of the trail overlooking the town. Wiebe's legacy lives on with the trail he started, the aim of which was to provide a recreational outlet close to town.

Be sure to look up on every hike.

I rated this hike "moderate" for its middling length, rocky trail conditions, and 1,300-foot elevation gain. The hike is a great blend of strenuous hiking, with periodic steep sections, and relaxing vistas and stopping points. The hike can be sunny and exposed in the middle section where it emerges from the tree cover and overlooks town. Bring plenty of water and sunscreen.

JUD WIEBE MEMORIAL TRAIL

BLUFF NATURE TRAIL—ALAMOSA NATIONAL WILDLIFE REFUGE

35

Rating	Easy
Round-Trip Distance	2.1 miles
Elevation Gain	120 feet
Round-Trip Time	1 hour
Maps	Alamosa National Wildlife Refuge
Main Attraction	Nature, different ecosystems, and easy access

COMMENT: An easy nature hike close to the San Luis Valley's largest town. Hikers will enjoy views of the Sangre de Cristo Range and the gorgeous San Luis Valley wetlands.

GETTING THERE: Note that Google Maps struggles to find this trailhead. The standard route on Google Maps tried to take me through private property and closed roads.

Left: Sandhill cranes congregate each fall in the San Luis Valley. **Right:** A sea of 8-foot-tall fall grasses.

Mount Blanca and the rest of the Sangre de Cristo Range make cameos on this hike.

From Alamosa, drive east on US 160 for 8 miles. Turn right (south) onto Valley Vista Boulevard. Drive for 1.5 miles, then turn right (south) on County Road 8. Drive west on CR 8 on the wide, smooth dirt road, then turn left after 2 miles onto 116 Road. Drive south for 5 miles, until turning right on the scenic drive. There are signs pointing toward the Bluff Trail. Follow the gorgeous road around the ridge to the marked Bluff Nature Trail Trailhead.

TRAILHEAD: The Bluff Nature Trail Trailhead is not much more than a pullout by a gate. Follow signage instructions and park out of the way of the gate.

THE ROUTE: From the Bluff Nature Trail Trailhead, hike south past the gate. The route follows an old road to a brilliant-yellow cottonwood grove. Cottonwood trees grow where water is readily available. This spot sits on a high-water table near the wetlands below. Enjoy the vibrant color in the grove and continue into a dense stand of greasewood.

Amid the greasewood, rabbitbrush, and fourwing saltbrush, grasses stand in various states of autumn transition. Follow the trail along the shallow ridge with views looking west to the San Juan Mountains.

Some of the peaks visible to the southwest are 13,179-foot Conejos Peak, to the south all the way to Bennett Peak, and Pintada Mountain to the north. Carry on southward amid the songs of western meadowlarks and into a low spot full of reeds and 8-foot-tall sand dropseed grasses.

A cottonwood island provides a burst of color.

At 0.9 mile, the trail bends to the right and borders a slope with plenty of evidence of water moving down the hill in rainy weather. The end of the trail is at just over 1 mile from the trailhead. Turn around and hike back to the trailhead. The hike back has views of 14,351-foot Mount Blanca, the fourth-highest peak in the Rocky Mountains and the third most prominent peak in Colorado. Blanca dominates the views in the southern part of the valley.

I rated this hike "easy" because of the flat, level sandy trail. The distance is short, and the elevation change is negligible.

I chose this hike for inclusion in this guide for a number of reasons. First, this is a local favorite of mine, close to my house, and is an excellent way to observe the unique hydrology and ecology of the San Luis Valley. This is a special place in the state. Second, this valley is one of the most incredible places in the state to see wildlife.

Fall in the San Luis Valley is a hotspot of animal migration. The sandhill cranes stop over in the valley each spring and fall. On my brief hike, I spotted a garter snake, sandhill cranes, a red fox, a jackrabbit, and soaring bald eagles. This hike is included in this guide for the nature lovers.

THE SAN LUIS VALLEY ("THE VALLEY") has numerous easy hikes with vibrant towns adjacent for a post-hike meal. For another easy hike replete with wildlife, check out the Monte Vista National Wildlife Refuge Meadowlark Nature Trail.

For dense fall color, one to two weeks after the mountain colors have peaked, hike the state wildlife areas along the Rio Grande. Pay attention to rules about access here, as you often need a valid fishing or hunting license to access these areas legally. But the beauty along the Rio in fall is unrivaled.

BLUFF NATURE TRAIL—ALAMOSA NATIONAL WILDLIFE REFUGE

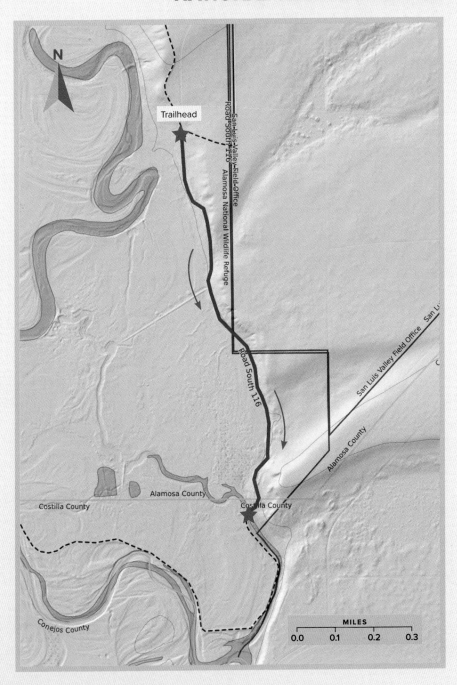

MOLAS PASS TO THE ANIMAS RIVER

36

Rating	Moderate to the river overlook, difficult to the river
Round-Trip Distance	4.7 miles to the overlook, 9 miles to the river
Elevation Gain	1,000 feet to the overlook, 2,200 to the river
Round-Trip Time	4–6 hours
Maps	Trails Illustrated 140: Weminuche Wilderness
Main Attraction	A breathtaking hike with panoramas of the Weminuche Wilderness, the Needle Mountains, and the Grenadier Range

COMMENT: This is a hike that offers options on length and difficulty, and the beauty of the rugged wilderness area and the fall color is unavoidable. The full hike carries you to the Animas River, and if you time it right, you might catch a view of the Durango and Silverton Narrow Gauge Railroad.

The Animas River winds through the wilderness. Photo by Jeff Golden

COLORADO'S BEST HIKES FOR FALL COLORS

The color gets more and more dense the closer you get to the river. Photo by Jeff Golden

GETTING THERE: From Silverton, head south out of town on State Highway 110. Merge onto US 550 and drive south for 5 miles. The trailhead will be on your left (the east side of the road) between mile markers 66 and 65. The dirt trailhead on the side of the road is marked with a brown sign that reads "Molas Lake Molas Trail."

TRAILHEAD: The Molas Trailhead parking area is a large pullout with parking directly off the highway. The trail leaves the parking area on an unmarked but well-trodden path to the south, leaving from the middle of the parking area.

THE ROUTE: From the Molas Trail parking area, hike south for 0.2 mile to meet up with the Colorado Trail. Turn left (east) on the Colorado Trail. At 0.35 mile, stay straight on the Colorado Trail as the trail descends. There are trails in this

Molas Pass to the Animas River

area that lead north to the private property around Molas Lake. Stay on the main Colorado Trail.

The upper reaches of the trail here present panoramic views over a verdant meadow while slowly descending into the valley below. At 0.65 mile, the trail switchbacks steeper down with some aspens and a roaring cascade below the trail. In fall, the grassy meadow is full of color.

Continue through a flatter area before beginning to descend in a meadow ringed with aspens. Nearing 2 miles into your hike, you will begin to find overlooks that provide a view over the remaining descent, the river, the train tracks, and the sheer peaks across the river.

Continuing through the aspens, the trail reaches an exposed overlook at 2.4 miles. This is a great point to take a break, enjoy the views, and turn around to climb back to the car.

The peaks visible across the valley are the spectacular Grenadier Range. The pointed peak is Mount Garfield, a 13er. The peaks are part of the Weminuche Wilderness, the largest wilderness area in the state. The Weminuche Wilderness was designated a wilderness area in 1975 and expanded in 1980 and 1993, offering up just shy of five hundred thousand acres of wilderness.

If you time your hike right, you might catch a view of the historic Durango and Silverton Narrow Gauge Railroad train. The train runs 45 scenic miles between Durango and Silverton and ferries tourists and hikers through this majestic canyon, along the Animas River. The track is a narrow 3 feet wide, and the train has been in operation since 1881. Two train stops allow hikers access into the Needle Mountains and are often used by climbers trying to access the 14ers around Chicago Basin: Windom, Eolus, and Sunlight Peaks.

AFTER THE TURN-BACK POINT ON THIS HIKE, the trail continues all the way down to the river. The descent is steep, full of switchbacks, and has great aspen cover. The trail goes all the way down to the Animas River, making the round-trip distance 9 miles with an elevation gain of 2,200 feet back to the trailhead.

If you choose to descend to the river, make sure everyone in your group is up for the challenge of climbing back to the trailhead. The views at the bottom are majestic and well worth the effort of the descent and climb back to the trailhead.

MOLAS PASS TO THE ANIMAS RIVER

BEAR CREEK TRAIL—TELLURIDE

37

Rating	Moderate
Round-Trip Distance	4.6 miles
Elevation Gain	1,200 feet
Round-Trip Time	3 hours
Maps	Trails Illustrated 141: Telluride, Silverton, Ouray, Lake City
Main Attraction	Aspens, peaks, and a waterfall

COMMENT: The Bear Creek Trail departs right from the streets of Telluride, culminating in a cascading waterfall surrounded by peak views and fall color. A gradual climb, the trail still clocks in at 4.6 miles round trip and climbs over 1,000 feet.

GETTING THERE: The trail begins at the end of South Pine Street in downtown Telluride. From "main street" (CO 145, Colorado Avenue), turn south on Pine Street and continue until the road ends after the river crossing and near the Riverside Condominiums. Follow parking regulations as there are no-parking areas and metered

Left: A carpet of leaves ushers hikers higher. **Right:** The middle portion of the hike is full of both color and big views of peaks above.

sites. There is no parking allowed at the condominium complex adjacent to the trailhead. There are parking garages in town that may be your best bet. This is also a residential area, so be wary of blocking anyone's driveway and respect residents' privacy.

TRAILHEAD: The Bear Creek Trail begins at a large brown sign adjacent to the condominiums at the end of Pine Street. No parking s allowed at the trailhead. Find a legal place to park in town and walk to the trailhead.

THE ROUTE: From the trailhead by the condominiums, hike up the dirt hill adjacent to the condos. Follow the wide dirt path to the Bear Creek Preserve sign (support your local land conservation nonprofit!). Hike up the wide dirt path, enshrined in aspens.

Bear Creek Falls.

This can be a popular trail, so navigate the crowds as you climb. It is steeper at first before easing up a bit after the first 0.5 mile. Keep climbing through periodic open views and continuing into a mixed forest. Ignore the minor social trails down to the river and continue on the well-established Bear Creek Trail, unless you packed a lunch, as the trail is replete with unofficial, social picnic spots by the river.

At 1.9 miles, the trail climbs steeper. Look for your first views of the falls but be content in the meantime with emerging vistas of towering cliffs beyond the aspens. At the intersection with the Wasatch Trail, stay left to continue toward the waterfalls on a less-established trail. The social trail is steep and narrow as you climb toward a large boulder at 2.3 miles. Closer views of the falls are possible by carefully scrambling up the boulder. Return the way you came.

The jagged peaks rising above the trail to the east are La Junta (13,465 feet) and Wasatch (13,555 feet) Peaks. The lower falls are the destination for this hike, but if you choose to continue, there is also an upper Bear Creek Falls. The lower falls are about 70 feet tall and provide a number of beautiful views.

Looking back down the valley toward Telluride.

This trail is made available to the public via a partnership with the San Miguel Conservation Foundation and the town of Telluride. The San Miguel Conservation Foundation acquired the 320 acres that make up the Bear Creek Preserve and donated the land to the city in 1995. The Great Outdoors Colorado Trust Fund also provided funding for the project. This unique partnership between private and public organizations has given us all the opportunity to enjoy this hike close to town.

I rated this trail "moderate" due to its 4.6-mile round-trip distance and the 1,200-foot elevation gain. The trail itself is wide and well-traveled with sure footing until the spur trail heading closer to the falls. There, the trail is more overgrown and less maintained. Be careful around the falls and rocks if you choose to explore closer to the water.

BEAR CREEK TRAIL—TELLURIDE

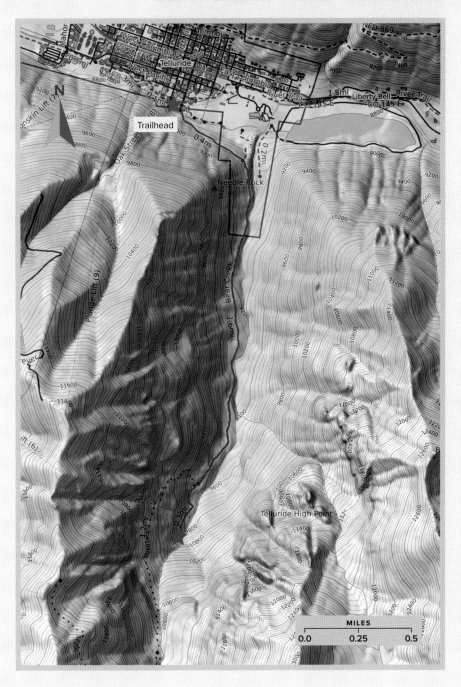

CLEAR LAKE TRAIL

38

Rating	Easy
Round-Trip Distance	1.75 miles
Elevation Gain	100 feet
Round-Trip Time	2 hours
Maps	Trails Illustrated 141: Telluride, Silverton, Ouray, Lake City
Main Attraction	Red and yellow aspens

COMMENT: With abundant camping and hiking at the nearby Silver Jack Reservoir, this hike is an excellent option for an easy day hike to beautiful ponds ringed by aspens turning shades of orange, red, and yellow.

Cattle graze below a sea of aspen and cliffs above.

Note that while Silver Jack Reservoir is an excellent choice for fall color hiking, these small lakes hold water more reliably than the often-low Silver Jack Reservoir.

GETTING THERE: From Ridgway, drive north out of town on US 550 for 2.1 miles. Turn east onto County Road 10. Follow CR 10 for 25 miles. The road is a well-maintained dirt road that climbs east over Owl Creek Pass with views of the incredible Cimarron Ridge. Descending from Owl Creek Pass, CR 10 becomes Route 860.

Continue on until you approach Silver Jack Reservoir. Stay left and follow signs to the reservoir. Turn left at the T junction, taking Forest Service Road 858 for 2.4 miles. Turn right onto Rowdy Lake Road (FR 838) and continue on for 1 mile. The last miles on FR 838 are more challenging and will require higher clearance or careful driving.

Multicolored aspens above Clear Lake.

TRAILHEAD: The Clear Lake/Rowdy Lake Trailhead provides parking and restroom facilities right next to a small lake.

THE ROUTE: This easy hike begins on the shores of Rowdy Reservoir, skirting the left side of it and heading through a gate to enter a flat, open meadow with large old aspen trees along the edge. The lake and surrounding area are ringed in golden aspens.

Continue down the easy trail, looking east to the sheer cliffs rising out of the trees. Cows often graze in the meadows you will pass through. At 0.5 mile, cross a shallow stream, hopping rocks to cross and continue to your destination, Clear Lake, at 0.75 mile.

Clear Lake is a small pond noteworthy for its dense groves of aspens that turn red and orange, mixed in with the more typical brilliant gold. Social trails abound around the collection of lakes and marshland. Explore as much as you like, even heading east to get a closer look at the cliffs and fiery color. Turn back and return the way you came.

On the walk back, views of Redcliff and Courthouse Mountain make for a scenic backdrop to the colorful valley. Courthouse Mountain is the distinctive 12,152-foot

The aspens here are prone to turning red and orange.

peak with jagged ridges and a large dome. The peak lies within the Uncompahgre Wilderness and is visible prominently on the drive to the trailhead from the west.

I rated this hike "easy" due to its short length, level slope, and easy footing. This is a great short hike for anyone staying at any of the local campgrounds.

WHY DO SOME ASPENS TURN RED? Tree leaves contain a number of different compounds that reflect different wavelengths of light. The most well-known is chlorophyll, the green pigment that allows plants to photosynthesize. As fall approaches, days become shorter and temperatures drop, triggering trees to slow down the production of chlorophyll. Most aspen trees turn golden yellow. With chlorophyll out of the picture, another substance in the leaves, called carotene, reflects yellow light, giving trees their distinctive golden color in the fall. But why do some trees turn red or orange? Aspens with higher acid levels in their sap, caused by higher sugar contents, have more anthocyanins in their leaves. Anthocyanins are the compounds that reflect red light and are more dominant in leaves after chlorophyll production stops. Some trees are genetically predisposed to turn red but will not necessary be red year to year. Warm, bright days with cool nights above freezing seem to stimulate the red color change the most.

CLEAR LAKE TRAIL

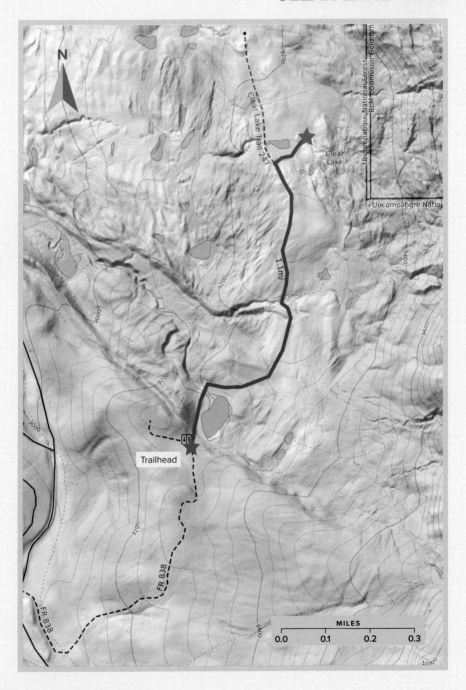

CRYSTAL LAKE— OURAY

39

Rating	Difficult
Round-Trip Distance	2.1 miles
Elevation Gain	1,000 feet
Round-Trip Time	3 hours
Maps	Trails Illustrated 141: Telluride, Ouray, Silverton, Lake City
Main Attraction	Aspen panoramas

COMMENT: A challengingly steep, sometimes difficult-to-follow trail that leads to tree line and provides spectacular views over one of the most colorful parts of the state, the north end of the Million Dollar Highway from Durango to Ouray.

GETTING THERE: From Ouray, travel south on Highway 550 out of town 6.5 miles to Crystal Lake. The readily visible roadside lake has easy parking and usually plenty of people taking in the fall colors.

One of the less-steep sections of the Crystal Lake Trail.

TRAILHEAD: Hayden Trailhead Crystal Lake is a roadside pullout next to the lake. Park off on the shoulder and don't block traffic. This is a busy area with cars speeding by. Use caution.

THE ROUTE: Start on the north side of Crystal Lake, a spring-fed lake that surely will have plenty of people hiking the easy loop around the water. Hike west along the north side of the lake to the trail junction. Head uphill. At 0.3 mile, the trail threads between two dry creek beds before climbing wooden stairs and getting increasingly steeper.

There are pleasant overlooks at the 0.5-mile mark (500 feet of elevation gain from the trailhead) and the 0.6-mile mark (600 feet). Switchback and continue to climb through dense aspen stands, watching the

The view of Crystal Lake from high on the ultra-steep trail.

height of the trees shrink as you approach tree line.

After 1.1 miles, at the 10,900-foot mark (1,200 feet of gain from the car), the trail skirts a dry, rocky creek bed with majestic views and an unparalleled feeling of vertical exposure as you peer back on the valley you just climbed. Catch your breath and head back down the way you came. Take your time on the descent, as this one is full of loose rock on a steep trail that is very tough on the knees.

The steep peak you are climbing is Hayden Mountain North, while the colorful mountains across the valley are Abrams Mountain and Brown Mountain, from north to south. This area of the state is filled with incredible, and incredibly steep, hikes such as this one. The nearby town of Ouray shows just how steep the topography is around these parts of the San Juan Mountains. Ouray is nestled in a box canyon and is renowned year-round as one of Colorado's most entertaining outdoor playgrounds, regardless of your sport of choice.

I rated this hike "difficult" because of its extreme grade. Despite a short distance, the trail climbs 1,000 feet in that short span. The trail is built well with logs

The views across the valley are colorful and grand.

Red and yellow shrubbery under a towering aspen canopy.

forming steps on some of the steeper sections and switchbacks tackling others. But there are still sections that feel very steep. As such, there are sections of loose rock and dirt that make the descent in particular rather harrowing. Be careful and take your time on the way up and down. As you get above tree line, watch for rockfall coming from the steep and loose slopes above.

Fishing for a variety of trout species is available in Crystal Lake. The small lake, more of a pond really, is a popular pullover point for motorists traveling the "Million Dollar Highway": US 550 between Ouray and Durango. Expect the crowds of people fishing and taking photos of the incredible fall color to thin out considerably as soon as you start climbing the slopes of Hayden Peak.

CRYSTAL LAKE—OURAY

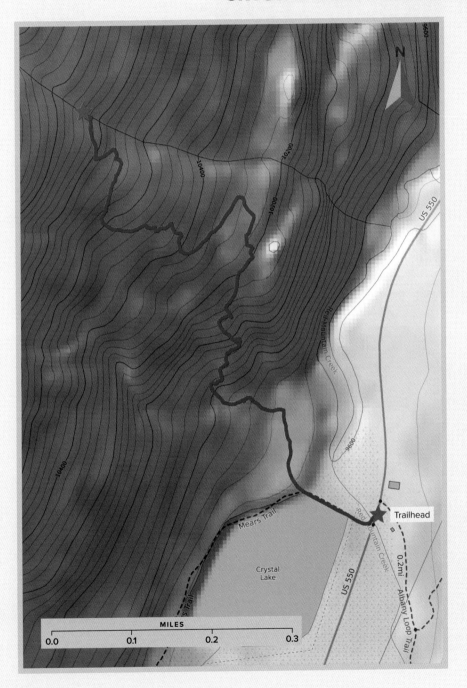

MOUNT SNEFFELS ARBORGLYPHS— DALLAS DIVIDE

40

Rating	Easy
Round-Trip Distance	3.5 miles
Elevation Gain	430 feet
Round-Trip Time	3 hours
Maps	Trails Illustrated 141: Telluride, Silverton, Ouray, Lake City
Main Attraction	Aspens below Mount Sneffels

COMMENT: Mount Sneffels may be the most beautiful mountain in Colorado, in this hiker's opinion. This easy trail traverses meadows and passes through old and new aspens alike, culminating in historic arborglyphs.

Old-growth aspen under the jagged Uncompahgres.

GETTING THERE: From Ridgway, drive west on CO 62 for 4.3 miles. Turn left (south) onto County Road 7. Follow the well-maintained (though narrow) dirt road for just shy of 9 miles until approaching the Blue Lakes Trailhead area. The drive there, in and of itself, is spectacularly scenic.

TRAILHEAD: There is plenty of parking at the popular Blue Lakes Trailhead (and many incredible hiking options). But if able, continue on the road to the small parking lot at the west end of the parking area.

THE ROUTE: Your hike starts at the small pullout where CR 7 ends. Hike a gradual rise through a dark old-growth mixed forest. At 0.7 mile, pass through some of the largest aspens around until you enter the open and secluded Cocan Flats. This high mountain meadow, lined by aspens on one

The Sneffels Range from Cocan Flats.

side and fir trees on the other, often has cattle grazing and enjoying the views north (give them a wide berth and respect them as you would any large, dangerous animal). Follow the trail, skirting the right side of the meadow. Just shy of your 1-mile mark, stay left to continue on the Dallas Trail and climb out of Cocan Flats. Pass through a young aspen grove and descend gently through a mixed forest as you leave the flats. At the 1.6-mile mark, you will run into a fence and some views opening to the valley below. Pay attention to the large old-growth aspens around you. I was able to easily observe the carvings of passersby from the 1940s. The real show is on the way back to your car, as you return the way you came with fantastic views of the incredible Mount Sneffels massif rising above Cocan Flats in a flourish of yellow, red, and orange.

Arborglyphs dating from 1948.

Mount Sneffels is the large dome-shaped peak with a pointed precipice at the very top, visible throughout the hike and the drive in. The peak is 14,155 feet tall and is primarily climbed from the south through Yankee Boy Basin, accessible via Ouray.

I rated this hike "easy" because of its stable footing, modest elevation gain, and moderate distance. When the trail climbs, the slopes are moderate and the footing sure.

The classic 1969 film *True Grit* was filmed in nearby Ridgway, Colorado. The scenic ridge featured in this hike is occasionally visible in the John Wayne classic film, and the town nearby has a number of movie-themed parks and a restaurant for western film aficionados.

ARBORGLYPHS ARE THE CULTURALLY SIGNIFICANT TREES across the state that bear carvings made by people who passed through the woods long ago. These are not the run-of-the-mill "Ed was here 2022" defacings. Respect the historic trees and do not make new carvings on trees. These are culturally significant trees from early settlers, Native peoples, and laborers using the Forest Service lands. Many arborglyphs were carved by Hispano, Basque, and Greek immigrants in the state, particularly in the San Juan Mountains. These hard-working laborers came looking for work and found it in the high meadows across the state tending to sheep. This life was often lonely. Homesick carvings across the state feature etchings of lost loves, sheep, and scenes from far away homes. On the hike here along the Dallas Divide, names like "Francisco" and "Chavez" are clearly visible just steps from the trail. For more information on arborglyphs across the state, books such as Andrew Gulliford's *The Wooly West* are great resources for those looking to learn more about this fascinating art in the woods. Catch them while you can. Some of the oldest carvings are on the largest trees, which are reaching the end of their lifespans due to age, climate change, and disease.

MOUNT SNEFFELS ARBORGLYPHS— DALLAS DIVIDE

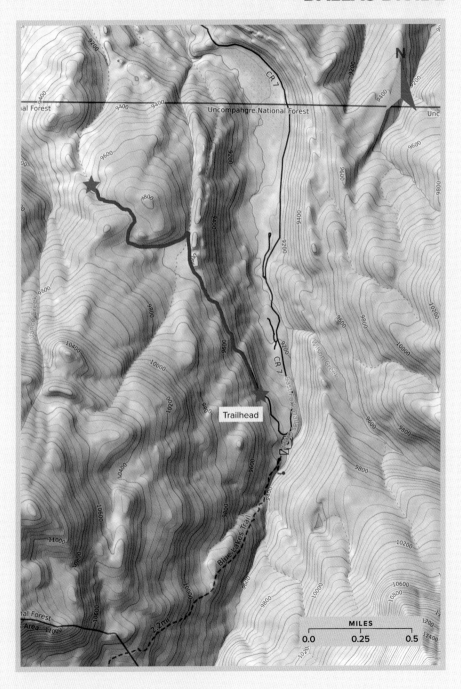

GREAT SAND DUNES NATIONAL PARK

41

Rating	Easy
Round-Trip Distance	1–3 miles
Elevation Gain	Negligible
Round-Trip Time	1–2 hours
Maps	Trails Illustrated 138: Sangre de Cristo Mountains
Main Attraction	Sand dunes

COMMENT: One of the most incredible, and unique, places in Colorado, the Great Sand Dunes National Park is worth a visit in every season. The autumn brings color to the aspens and cottonwoods on the ever-changing creek bed and fewer visitors than during the spring runoff season.

GETTING THERE: From Alamosa, the biggest town in the San Luis Valley, head east on Highway 160 for a little over 14 miles. Look for the brown signs directing you toward the national park. Turn left (north) on CO 150 and continue on for 18 miles to the national park entrance. Pay the entrance fee and continue on for 1 mile, past the visitor center, turning left at the small brown sign directing you toward the dunes/picnic area.

Left: Bring the kids! **Right:** Sand under a canopy of cottonwoods.

Cottonwoods cling to the edges of the dunefield.

TRAILHEAD: The main Great Sand Dunes Picnic Area Trailhead can get crowded. It has multiple shower facilities, bathrooms, and parking in the lot and along the road. Pay attention to no-parking signs.

THE ROUTE: From the parking area, there are multiple bridges and boardwalks to the creek bed. This is a bit of a self-directed hike, but it all begins by crossing the willow thickets between the parking area and the Medano Creek flats. Follow the creek upstream (to the east) for the best color in the cottonwoods, willows, and aspens that grow along the sides of the creek bed. The creek bed before you is an incredibly diverse place that changes with each month of the year.

From the winter snows and deep freeze to the spring runoff (replete with the closest thing Colorado gets to a beach party: waves, sun, and surf), to the summer heat, and finally the fall color and chill in the valley air, the Great Sand Dunes is a truly unique place that needs to be seen. Hike as far upstream as you'd like or climb the dunes for a different view (and added difficulty). Climbing sand is harder than climbing maintained trails, and be warned that, on a hot day, the sand can be scorching. Sand boards are available for rent outside the park entrance, but you may

Great Sand Dunes National Park

find that the views of the peaks of the Sangre de Cristo range towering above the dunes and the yellow on the creek bed are more than enough fun for an afternoon.

Medano Creek runs down into the San Luis Valley from Medano Pass. The National Park Service keeps track of the creek's flow with a regularly updated graph on their website. Not all fall years will feature a running creek at the parking area, depending on summer and fall rain totals in the valley, but if water is what you're after, the National Park Service can advise how far up the Medano Pass Primitive Road a capable four-wheel-drive vehicle has to drive. The Medano Pass Primitive Road passes above the dune field into the Grand Sand Dunes National Preserve. The preserve contains a chunk of the alpine mountains and is full of alpine lakes, aspen stands, and rugged steep trails.

Great Sand Dunes National Park was established as a national monument in 1932 and then officially converted to a national park in 1994. While the dunefield may look confined to the area visible from the parking lot, the dunes cover more than 30 square miles and are among the tallest in North America. The dunes were formed over the course of millions of years by the valley's strong winds from the west blowing and depositing sand against the prominent Sangre de Cristo Mountains. Note that this is one of the darkest night skies in America. Stay the night locally for crisp air and views of the Milky Way in all its majesty.

The northern ridges of the Blanca massif over the dunefield.

GREAT SAND DUNES NATIONAL PARK

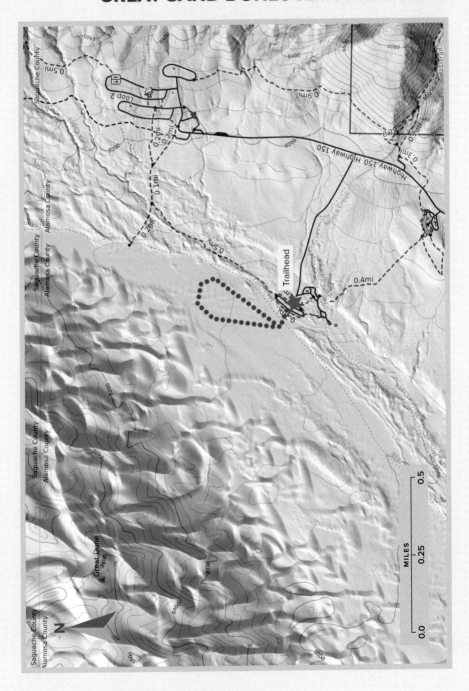

HANDIES PEAK— AMERICAN BASIN

42

Rating	Difficult
Round-Trip Distance	5.25 miles
Elevation Gain	2,500 feet
Round-Trip Time	5 hours
Maps	Trails Illustrated 141: Telluride, Silverton, Ouray, Lake City
Main Attraction	Tundra ablaze in color

COMMENT: One of the "easier" 14ers, Handies Peak is an island in the sky in one of the most scenic parts of the state. Hiking above tree line in the fall provides more stable weather, cooler temperatures, fewer crowds, and tundra plants ablaze in red and yellow.

Fall majesty on the approach to American Basin.

Lichen far above tree line.

GETTING THERE: From Lake City, drive south on Colorado Highway 149 out of town for 2.5 miles. Turn right on County Road 30. Drive past Lake San Cristobal amid private property. The paved road soon gives way to an easy gravel road before getting rougher around the Cataract Gulch site. Soon after passing the Mill Creek Campground, stay right on County Road 30. Four-wheel-drive and high clearance are musts from here to the trailhead (another 8 miles of slow going). Turn left on County Road 12 to the American Basin Trailhead. The road gets significantly more difficult in this last 0.9 mile to the official trailhead, with rock steps and boulder obstacles. Park where you are comfortable and hike the difference.

TRAILHEAD: The American Basin Trailhead is one of the most incredible places I've ever slept with a car right next to me. Truly, if you can make a night of it, do it. The official trailhead (11,600 feet) can be inaccessible for all but the most well-equipped drivers. So, don't get stuck out here, and hike to the trailhead if you can't reach it by car. No restroom facilities exist.

Handies Peak—American Basin

American Basin from below.

THE ROUTE: Regardless of where you were able to park, trek to the trailhead at roughly 11,600 feet elevation. Mileages in this description begin at the trailhead. Sign in to the trail register and climb along the trail up the gully on the west side of Handies Peak.

At 1.1 miles and roughly 12,400 feet, stay left at the junction with the Grouse Gulch Trail. The trail curves east and switchbacks up to Sloan Lake, at the base of the 13,727-foot American Peak. This is a great spot to take a break before the next push toward the summit.

When you're ready, descend from the lake through talus and head east, climbing away from the lake and into a rocky cirque where you will be able to see most of the route remaining above you to the north. At 2.5 miles and roughly 13,500 feet, you will reach the saddle between Handies Peak and the unnamed point to the south. Continue up the steep final push to 14,048 feet at just under 3 miles from the trailhead.

The views around the basin are a panorama of orange and gold tundra foliage, waiting for the coming snow. The peak can be quite chilly, so pack a jacket for your summit celebration. Return the way you came.

I rated this hike "difficult" because of the typical hazards of navigating a high-elevation hike. The mileage is long, and the elevation gains are aggressive. There are very steep sections of trail, loose rock, and thin air. Take care to acclimate to high altitudes before attempting a high-elevation climb. Know the symptoms of altitude sickness (dizziness, disorientation, headache, nausea) and turn back if needed. Be conservative. Also, while this route does not have as much risk as some of the other 14ers, watch for rockfall, particularly on the scree fields. Bring plenty of sunscreen and dress for a cold alpine climate at the top. Watch the weather coming in across the surrounding ridges and know that high on a peak is not where you want to be when weather moves in. Conditions can change quickly and require vigilant observation and trip planning.

Looking down from the final summit approach, back into American Basin.

HANDIES PEAK—AMERICAN BASIN

OPAL LAKE

Rating	Moderate
Round-Trip Distance	2.8 miles
Elevation Gain	520 feet
Round-Trip Time	2.5 hours
Maps	Trails Illustrated 142: South San Juan, Del Norte
Main Attraction	Mature forests, vibrant colors, and a unique pond

COMMENT: This is a gem of a hike, with opal-colored waters, tall aspens, and dramatic cliffs. A great hike for the family!

GETTING THERE: From Pagosa Springs, drive east on US Highway 160. Turn right (south) onto US 84 east and continue for 8.7 miles. Turn left on Blanco Basin Road (CR 326). Continue for 6.2 miles and stay left to keep on Blanco Basin Road for

Approaching the lake.

The contrast between the lake, the aspens, and the cliffs is breathtaking.

another 2.6 miles. Follow signs for Opal Lake for another 1.2 miles before turning right onto Fish Creek Road. Turn right onto Fish Creek Road and continue for 4 miles to the Opal Lake Trailhead. The road is dirt but smooth and easily passable.

TRAILHEAD: The Opal Lake Trailhead is a small dirt parking area with room for fifteen or so cars.

THE ROUTE: From the Opal Lake Trailhead, hike gently uphill in a mature mixed forest. The trail climbs a dirt (or mud) trail through tall aspens and pine trees, past a small pond with the characteristically milky-green water that gives this hike its name.

Continue to climb through a beautiful Douglas fir and aspen forest. The hike's climb is steady but not overly steep. The grade is doable for the whole family. At just over 0.5 mile, tackle the first of multiple creek crossings.

Climb through the last steep push under tall, skinny aspen trees, into an open meadow at 0.9 mile. Take a moment to catch your breath and spy the steep cliffs and panoramic aspen color above. The trail levels out from here to the lake and is a joy to hike.

At 1 mile, stay straight to continue on Opal Lake Trail. The trail crosses the creek multiple times in this section in backcountry conditions. Expect to walk narrow logs laid across shallow streams.

Stay left at the trail junction sign to once again head toward Opal Lake. This final stretch of trail has amazing views over the aspens, willows, and cliffs above.

At 1.3 miles, the trail reaches the lake. Opal Lake is a distinctive milky-green color. The placid green waters, under the unnamed cliffs, ridges, and peaks above are a gorgeous destination for the hike. Take some time to enjoy the view of these cliffs, part of the San Juan Wilderness south of Wolf Creek Pass. When you're ready, return the way you came back to the trailhead.

Opal Lake beneath a sea of aspens.

I rated this hike "moderate" because it does climb steadily for a mile and the footing is far from flat and easy. The steeper nature of this trail and the dirt footing can make this trail muddy if you hike it during or after a rain. But this hike is, all in all, low in mileage and altogether a modest elevation gain. My six-year-old tackled this hike with no issues (besides some moderate complaining about the "scary" creek crossings at the top).

This hike is obviously named after the milky-green waters of the lake and draining creek. The mineral-rich waters give the water of the pond an opal-colored hue.

This entire area of the San Juan Mountains is rich in minerals and geothermal activity. The town of Pagosa Springs, and the adjacent San Luis Valley over Wolf Creek Pass, are rich in mineral hot springs. Take some time after your hike to soak your sore muscles in one of the local pools.

OPAL LAKE

POTATO LAKE

Rating	Easy
Round-Trip Distance	3.5 miles
Elevation Gain	265 feet
Round-Trip Time	2 hours
Maps	Trails Illustrated 140: Weminuche Wilderness
Main Attraction	An easy hike to a placid lake, ringed with color

COMMENT: A fun, easy-going option for those enjoying the fall around Durango, this trek takes hikers up a gentle slope to a lake full of rising fish.

GETTING THERE: From Durango, drive north on US 550 for around 28 miles. Cross Cascade Creek (look for the green road sign marking the creek) and turn right onto the wide shoulder area that turns into Lime Creek Road. Climb the rough road for 2.8 miles to a roadside marsh. The road will require some high clearance on your vehicle. The trailhead is across the road from the large marshy lake.

TRAILHEAD: The trailhead for this hike is unmarked but is directly across from the lake. There are small parking spots to pull into, perpendicular to the road. The road in requires high clearance.

THE ROUTE: From the trailhead parking, look for two small wooden fence posts. The trail climbs through a lush aspen forest across a rocky surface. The colorful foliage here is thick, and the fluttering of the quaking aspen leaves is audible in the breeze.

The climb to the lake on a misty morning.
Photo by Jeff Golden

Potato Lake ringed with color. Photo by Jeff Golden

Continue to climb the gradual slope as the trees open up for occasional views of Engineer Mountain and colorful hills carpeted with aspens. The trail continues to climb steadily on a rocky substrate as it turns to a more easterly heading and follows a brook running through a drainage 20 feet below the trail. Join the creek at around 0.5 mile from the trailhead and keep climbing.

The trail begins to level out as you approach the lake. Pass some small beaver ponds. Climb the last small push to the lake to a rocky shoreline with plenty of fantastic spots to rest, eat lunch, or cast a line. The lake is at 1.1 miles from the trailhead.

Loop around the lake on the trail in whichever direction looks appealing to you and your group. The walk around the lake adds 0.7 mile to your round-trip total. Potato Hill rises above the north shore of the lake at a summit elevation of 11,871 feet.

Fly fishermen may want to pack in their gear and cast a line. On the day I hiked to Potato Lake, fish were rising all over the lake, and I was kicking myself for not packing my rod. On such a moderate hike to a healthy lake, fishing gear would be well worth the ounces in the pack.

I rated this hike "easy" because of its modest elevation gain and short mileage. The trail is rocky (like the road in), but the footing is stable and the grade mild enough. This is a great hike to take the whole family on.

To the north of the hike is the small town of Silverton. Silverton is an extremely isolated town in one of the most picturesque places in the state. Take a short detour north after your hike for a meal if you'd like.

Silverton forms the southern terminus of a magnificent stretch of US 550 dubbed the "Million Dollar Highway," so named because it reportedly cost $1 million per mile to construct. A part of the San Juan Skyway Scenic Byway, the road winds north to Ouray on the edges of cliffs and affords magnificent views in every direction. In the fall, this may be the most picturesque stretch of highway all of Colorado, if not the West.

POTATO LAKE

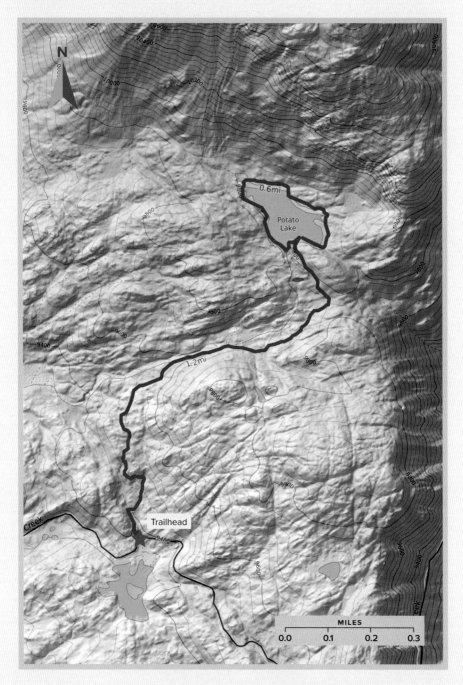

N

10400
10000
10200
9800
9600
9600
9400

0.6mi

Potato
Lake

10200

9800

9600

9800

9800

1.2mi

9800

9800

9600

9600

Creek

Trailhead

9400

9600

reek

MILES

| 0.0 | 0.1 | 0.2 | 0.3 |

YANKEE BOY BASIN

45

Rating	Easy
Round-Trip Distance	1.5 miles
Elevation Gain	481 feet
Round-Trip Time	2 hours
Maps	Trails Illustrated 141: Telluride, Silverton, Ouray, Lake City
Main Attraction	Alpine majesty replete with tundra fall colors

COMMENT: Yankee Boy Basin is one of Colorado's most incredible, easily accessible alpine basins. Combine the rugged Uncompahgre geography with tundra grasses alight in fall color, and this is a worthwhile adventure.

GETTING THERE: From Ouray, take Camp Bird Road to the Yankee Boy Basin area. On the south side of Ouray, there is a large bend on Highway 550. Across the highway from the large "See the Famous Box Canyon Falls" sign is a steep road climbing upward, toward the Ouray Ice Park. Pass the ice park and continue to climb on Camp Bird Road for 4.7 miles. This is an active mining road. Watch out for mining equipment, trucks, and falling rocks, and make sure you're comfortable driving narrow roads with no guard rails.

Stay right at the mine and continue on County Road 26 until it becomes Yankee Boy Basin Road. Stay right to climb the four-wheel-drive Yankee Boy Basin Road. From here on out, the road gets more and more difficult. Drive as high as you are comfortable and park in one of the designated pull-offs. The Wrights Lake Trailhead is 1.7 miles up the Yankee Boy Basin Road.

There are a number of locations in Ouray and surrounding towns that rent Jeeps and similarly capable off-road vehicles.

Colorful tundra grasses.

TRAILHEAD: The Wrights Lake Spur and Trailhead was not marked when I hiked it. But Google Maps has the turnoff clearly marked on the map.

THE ROUTE: From the Wright's Lake Spur and Trailhead, hike west on the narrow trail across the tundra. The trail meanders on the side of one of the basin's many piles of loose alpine rock, speckled with blazing-red undergrowth and stubby yellow willows clinging to the rocks. Bursts of orange lichen, while not a plant but rather a fascinating "combination organism" made up of symbiotic colonies of algae and bacteria, add to the stunning alpine scenery.

The trail clings to the edge of the steep hillside while climbing steadily. At 0.4 mile from the Wrights Lake Trailhead, triangular Wrights Lake sits at the base of a massive scree field that flows down like a glacier from the ridge connecting Mount Sneffels to the north and Gilpin Peak to the south. The lake is a fantastic place to marvel in the alien landscape of the alpine tundra.

After you've had your fill of alpine air, or caught your breath as it may be, hike northeast on the wide trail climbing away from the alpine tarn. At 0.75 mile from the trailhead, the trail climbs to the hike's high point and joins the jeep road. Take the meandering aggressive four-wheel-drive "road" back down to wherever you were able to park, a distance of 1.3 miles in total when you reach the Wrights Lake Spur and Trailhead.

Left: The trail clings to the edge as it winds its way up. **Right:** The alpine tarn at the base of Mount Sneffels.

Looking back down on the trail in this beautiful high-alpine paradise.

The entire cirque is ringed with rugged alpine peaks, permanent snowfields, and gorgeous fall color from the tundra plant community. The prominent peak at the northwest corner of the basin is 14,150-foot Mount Sneffels. Sneffels is as iconic as mountains get in Colorado, even making it onto a recent version of the Colorado driver's license.

Yankee Boy Basin is the most common route taken by those climbing the peak. Feel free to explore the trails farther up the basin before returning to your vehicle. It isn't very often that you can drive to such a picturesque alpine environment. As always in the tundra, stay on established trails as the plant communities at this elevation are very sensitive and often take decades just to grow a small amount.

I rated this hike "easy" because of the short distance and modest elevation gains. That being said, the drive in to the trailhead is anything but easy. Depending on how far up the road your vehicle can go, you may find yourself hiking 1.7 miles (and 1,000 vertical feet) to the Wrights Lake Spur and Trailhead. In that case, this hike could easily be seen as a "difficult" hike, especially for those not used to hiking at such high elevations.

YANKEE BOY BASIN

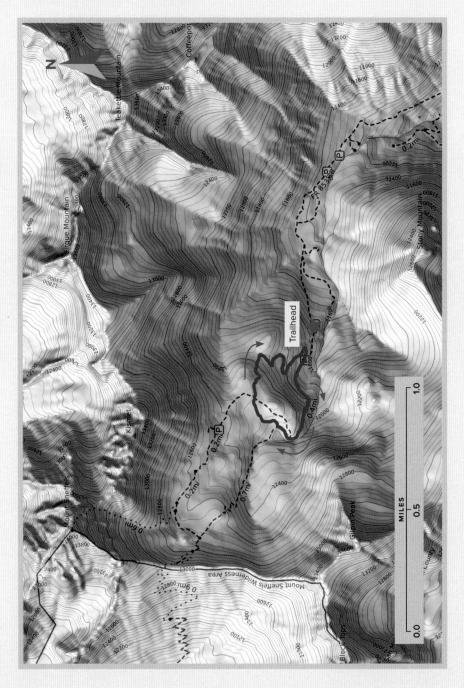

ACKNOWLEDGMENTS

I am grateful for the opportunity to ramble so widely around this state. Thank you to my wife and daughter for granting me the time to write this book over three years, knowing that I'm better in both roles at home when I am fresh off the trail, smelling like a rose, and advocating for a family trip to the hot springs.

Thank you to the CMC crew, Sarah and Jeff, for getting this book idea moving and across the finish line.

Thank you to the family and friends who inspired my love of trees and to all those who shared the trail with me. Thank you to Mario, Andres, Brian, and Katie in particular.

ABOUT THE AUTHOR

Matt Enquist lives in the San Luis Valley in majestic Southern Colorado. In addition to exploring the trails of Colorado, Matt has spent extensive time rambling in Alaska, Washington, California, Montana, Wisconsin, Michigan (Yoopers know), Wyoming, and Utah.

Matt grew up in the northern suburbs of Chicago before attending North Park University in Chicago, Illinois, to study creative writing. A 4,000-mile bicycle trip in 2008 reinvigorated a love for sleeping in the dirt. After school, Matt spent six years working in the outdoor industry before working in nonprofit land conservation and health care organizations. He has an awesome wife and daughter.

The author at camp. Photo by Mario Rangel

Recreate with
RIMS

Give back to the land you love with the **CMC RIMS** (Recreation Impact Monitoring System) mobile app: If you spot a downed tree, trail erosion, trash, or poor signage while you're exploring the places in this book, open the app and submit a quick report so that land managers can address the issue. Learn more and get started at cmc.org/RIMS.

cmc.org/RIMS

Illustration by Jesse Crock

Join Today.
Adventure Tomorrow.

The Colorado Mountain Club is the Rocky Mountain community for mountain education, adventure, and conservation. We bring people together to share our love of the mountains. We value our community and go out of our way to welcome and include all Coloradoans—from the uninitiated to the expert, there is a place for everyone here.

cmc.org